"*Girl on a Swing* lets us relax into God's grace and feel His love hold us high. Ahhh. Nancy's words let me be my imperfect self and still know that there is no wind strong enough to release me from my Father's grip. A book for all the seasons of your life."

KARON PHILLIPS GOODMAN

AUTHOR OF *ANOTHER FINE MESS, LORD!*

AND THE WOMAN'S GUIDE SERIES

"Nancy Kennedy has long been one of my favorite writers. But I think *Girl on a Swing* might be her best book yet! She writes with amazing humor, heart, and insight. *Girl on a Swing* soars!"

HEATHER KOPP

AUTHOR OF *ROAR: A CHRISTIAN FAMILY GUIDE*

*TO THE CHRONICLES OF NARNIA*

D0711079

# Girl on a Swing

## nancy kennedy

Multnomah® Publishers *Sisters, Oregon*

GIRL ON A SWING
published by Multnomah Publishers, Inc.

© 2006 by Nancy Kennedy
International Standard Book Number: 1-59052-729-1

Cover design by Brand Navigation
Cover image by Andrea Olsheskie / Getty Images

Italics in Scripture are the author's emphasis.
Unless otherwise indicated, Scripture quotations are from:
*The Holy Bible,* New International Version
© 1973, 1984 by International Bible Society,
used by permission of Zondervan Publishing House
Other Scripture quotations are from:
*The Message*
© 1993, 1994, 1995, 1996, 2000, 2001, 2002
Used by permission of NavPress Publishing Group
*New American Standard Bible* ® (NASB) © 1960, 1977, 1995
by the Lockman Foundation. Used by permission.
*The Amplified Bible* (AMP)
© 1965, 1987 by Zondervan Publishing House.
*The Amplified New Testament* © 1958, 1987 by the Lockman Foundation.
*Contemporary English Version* (CEV) © 1995 by American Bible Society

*Multnomah* is a trademark of Multnomah Publishers, Inc.,
and is registered in the U.S. Patent and Trademark Office.
The colophon is a trademark of Multnomah Publishers, Inc.

For information:
MULTNOMAH PUBLISHERS, INC.
601 N. LARCH STREET
SISTERS, OREGON 97759

06 07 08 09 10—10 9 8 7 6 5 4 3 2 1 0

*For Peggy, my favorite only sister.*
*Swing high, sistah!*

*Having loved His own…He loved them to the end.*

JOHN 13:1, NASB

# Table of Contents ✍

# Acknowledgments

Although the acknowledgments page is my favorite page of a book to write, it is also the most difficult. Where does one begin to acknowledge all those who, whether they play an active role or not, contribute to the making of a book? In what order should the names go? How personal should you get—and what if you leave somebody out, which undoubtedly you will?

But the truth is, I might type at my computer alone, but I cannot write without the help and support of many who surround me, uphold me, put up with me, and love me. That said, I could not have written this book without:

- Barry Kennedy, my best friend for more than thirty years, who has cheered me on in whatever I do and who "knows how I am" and loves me anyway. Bear, I think you're amazing. *Poof! You're a sandwich.*
- My daughters, Alison and Laura, or as I like to call them, "story fodder."
- Tara Bryant, a rare friend who knows the dirt. *Grace and sushi to you in abundance, my friend.*
- Steve Brown, the one I call my uncle-dad, who prays for me daily, encourages me often, lets me steal his wise words, and doesn't seem to tire of hearing about The Saga Thus Far.

- Martin Luther and the apostle Paul, for their radical teachings about grace.
- My church, Seven Rivers Presbyterian Church in Lecanto, Florida, especially my pastor, Ray Cortese. I am eternally grateful for the privilege of belonging to such a strange and wonderfully odd group of people who "get grace deeply to give it generously."
- My "sisters in the mess" and the Wearers of the Bracelets: Carol, Margaret, Patty, Angel, Laura, Tara, Diane. Thanks for the prayers and for being the "girls on the swing" along with me.
- Kashi "GOLEAN Crunch!" cereal with dried cranberries and fat-free vanilla pudding; my CD of rolling thunder and rain; soft, white Egyptian cotton sheets on my bed; and the leather chair by my back window where I meet with God.
- Mike Wright, a fellow writer, my first reader, best critic, and, most importantly, a brother in Christ.
- My co-workers at the *Citrus County Chronicle*, especially the publisher, Gerry Mulligan, for letting me write about my faith every week in my column, Grace Notes. Parts of this book have been adapted from my columns. *Bring on the cake!*
- The team at Multnomah Publishers, who has enthusiastically embraced both me and this book.
- Sherri Basham, quite possibly my loudest and definitely my most energetic cheerleader. *Bless your heart, darlin'.*
- Dave and Heather Kopp, for their years of being my champions.
- Donald Miller, for writing the book *Blue Like Jazz*. Reading it helped free something in me to write true truth about myself and about my faith.

- Saving the best for last—to the One whose smile I don't deserve and can't repay. I stand amazed in Your presence. Accept this book as an offering of my worship. Do with it as You please, my gracious God, merciful Savior, precious Redeemer, and sovereign Lord.

# Girl on a Swing

## Introduction

When I was about eighteen, I went to see a therapist. Not that anything terribly traumatic had happened to me, but everyday life without purpose or meaning can be traumatic, too.

Here's how I thought about life: You wake up, you do your stuff during the day, then you go to bed. Day after day, that's what you do. And then when you do that enough times, you eventually die. Maybe somewhere in there you get married once or twice, you have some kids, maybe go to Disney World or visit the Grand Canyon or meet Regis Philbin or go on *Oprah*, but mostly you don't do any of that. Mostly you just do your regular stuff until you die.

That's how I thought about life—I was marking time until I died, yet at the same time I was terrified of dying.

So I went to this therapist who promised he could help me find peace from the voices that haunted me and freedom from the sense of doom, the marking time until I died, that I couldn't seem to shake. I met with him once, and as I lay on his couch and talked and cried, he moved me into a fetal position and then told me everything that was wrong in my life was my father's fault, that somehow he hadn't shown me the love I needed and craved.

*As I lay on his couch and talked and cried, he moved me into a fetal position and then told me everything that was wrong in my life was my father's fault.*

I went home and told my dad what the therapist had said, and as soon as I did, I knew he was wrong. My dad looked at me and asked, "Is that what you think?"

I told him no; I didn't think that at all. But the man had a framed certificate on the wall of his office, and I assumed he could look inside me and pinpoint the source of my pain. He seemed to think I lacked a father's love, that what I longed for, curled up on his couch in a fetal position, was the perfect love of a parent, a love that fills up the empty spaces inside a young girl's life.

He was wrong, but he was right, too. He just got the fathers mixed up. It wasn't my dad's love I lacked. Even back then I knew that, as imperfect as he was and is, my dad loved me the best way he knew how. But the Father whose love I really wanted was the One who created me in His own image. My whole insides screamed, frantically, furiously, instinctively, to know Him and to be known by Him. I just didn't know that He was the One I wanted. No one told me, or if someone did, I didn't hear.

*The Father whose love I really wanted was the One who created me in His own image.*

Back then, I only knew that I wanted:

a life that didn't make me want to escape it.
a love that didn't make me feel empty the next morning.
a reason to get up and get dressed every day.

I wanted:

to be able to sleep without medicating myself,
to have my racing, troubling thoughts quieted
to be rid of my guilt and shame,
to be part of a community where I didn't feel so alone,
to find rest and security—and hope.


I wanted to not be afraid of dying—or of living. What I wanted back then was freedom, although I didn't know the word at the time.


❧

Here's the truth: I am ten years old. I've tried to explain this to my daughters, who are both in their twenties, but they just look at me and then at each other, conferring silently that it might be time to put me in a home. Or one will ask if I've changed my hormone patch this week.

They tend to think that women my age are grown-ups. Perhaps some are, but I think most of us are just ten-year-olds wearing constricting shapewear under our clothes, plucking at stray chin whiskers, and taking notes during Depends commercials.

I told my daughters that the reason a group of forty- or fifty-year-old women would spit off a bridge is because inside they're all only ten years old. Okay, maybe they're twelve or fourteen, but I don't think we're ever older than that.

*I think most of us are just ten-year-olds wearing constricting shapewear under our clothes, plucking at stray chin whiskers, and taking notes during Depends commercials.*

I've been thinking about this for a long time. For about a year now, I've been staring off and on at a greeting card on my desk. It shows the image of a girl on a swing, midflight. She's about nine or ten, maybe eight. Her face is tilted skyward, and she looks like she's utterly enjoying the experience of momentum and the feeling that she's flying.

I bought the card to send to a friend, but I kept it for myself. The message inside says, "Fly high. Hope the wind is always at your back." However, I didn't choose the card for the message, but for the image of the girl—I can't take my eyes off of it. The longer I study it, the more I realize that what I've known all along is true, that the girl on the swing, leaning back, gently and easily pumping her legs, closing her eyes while the wind blows through her hair, her entire being warmed by the sun—the longer I stare at that picture, the more I know that the girl is me.

She is not who I want to be or hope to be, but because of Jesus, she is me.

She is safe, and she is me. She is secure, and she is me. She is free and forgiven, she is her Father's delight, and in Christ, she is me.

She's you, too.

I've talked to enough women in the past few years to know that most of them don't believe that, and I'm talking longtime church ladies, those you would think believed that about themselves. But if I showed the card to an average group of women and announced, "This is you," some, thinking that I was joking, would laugh.

Most, however, would smile, but then they would divert their eyes. They would think, *I want to be her. I want to feel loved and safe and secure. I want to feel free. I want to turn my face toward heaven and experience God's smile, to know that I am His child and that there's nothing I can do to make Him want to push me out of a speeding car or regret that I'm his.*

A few of them would cry, if only inwardly, and they would breathe a silent prayer or make a wish that maybe someday, if they could just get their acts together, if they could be holier somehow or maybe if they would work on their motives and thought life, if they could try to be nicer to people, especially their families, maybe if they could be worthy of being a Christian—whatever that means—maybe if they could stop being self-centered, if they could do all that, or even make progress in just one area of their lives…then maybe God would let them be that girl, if only briefly.

Let me say this again. That girl on the swing, pumping her legs, holding on to the ropes as she glides with ease and delight: She is me, and if Christ has set you free, she is you.

> *She is safe, and she is me. She is secure,*
> *and she is me. She is free and forgiven,*
> *she is her Father's delight, and in Christ, she is me.*
> *She's you, too.*

Hear the Word of God:

"It is for freedom that Christ has set us free" (Galatians 5:1), the apostle Paul told the church at Galatia. Before that, Jesus told His followers that if He sets a person free, then that person is "free indeed" (John 8:36). And if Christ has set us free, if we're "free indeed," then shouldn't all God's children be out scrambling for swing sets and experiencing the holy wind of God at their backs, lifting them up toward the sun? Shouldn't we all swing to the sky, trying to touch the stars or the moon or the neighbor's mulberry tree, convinced that God is well pleased, swinging just for the sheer pleasure of it?

And if we should be doing that, then why aren't we?

At my church we often sing a simple song about "God has smiled on me." We sing that He has "set me free" and that He's been "good to me." It's so simple, so basic, yet so difficult a concept to grasp and to own and to live out because we don't believe that God smiles, at least not at us. Monkeys maybe, and babies most likely make Him smile, and otters in the Monterey Bay are awfully cute.

But God smiling at you and at me?

> *We don't believe God smiles, at least not at us.*
> *Monkeys maybe, and babies most likely make Him smile,*
> *and otters in the Monterey Bay are awfully cute.*
> *But God smiling at you and at me?*

Oh, but He does! This is the *Reader's Digest* condensed version of how it works: The Father smiles on Jesus, the only one to ever live a perfect, sinless life and the only one who ever obeyed the law of God to the last comma and semicolon. And if we belong to Him through faith, the Father smiles on us, too.

I'm not sure when I grasped that. I came to faith in Jesus when I was twenty-three, but for a long time after that, even though I knew I belonged to God, I didn't know I was loved by Him.

Not really.

Actually, it was more like, I knew He loved me, but only as long as I didn't screw up too badly. I lived with a sense that there's a line you can't cross—although I never knew where the line was—and if you crossed it, you would be next on God's to-do list: *Smite this one with postnasal drip and a bad haircut, and remember to say no to her next three prayers.*

But somewhere, somehow, I eventually grasped it: that, based solely on my relationship with Jesus, I live every moment under God's smile. I can't escape it—ever—because it has nothing to do with what I do or don't do, but has everything to do with the One who has redeemed me.

I know it deep in my knower.

It's what I longed to know as a child growing up in a happy home. It's what I longed to know at eighteen, lying on the therapist's couch, and at twenty-three, when God's Spirit captured my heart and drew me to the Savior's feet.

It's what we were meant to know, deeply, personally, intimately, profoundly.

It's what the Father longs for us to know.

> *Based solely on my relationship with Jesus, I live every moment under God's smile. I can't escape it—ever—because it has nothing to do with what I do or don't do, but has everything to do with the One who has redeemed me.*

Do you know it? I mean *really* know it? Not just saying you do because that's the correct answer and you figure everyone but you knows it and you don't want to be odd man out. I'm talking about when you've committed the same sin for the eleven millionth time, when you've called someone an expletive (if only in your thoughts), when you think the Bible is dry as dirt, when you're tempted to kiss the UPS guy and leave your husband to deal with the laundry and the kids, when your faith is cold and your temper is hot—do you know then, even at your lowest, ugliest moments, that God smiles on you?

Do you know that if you are His, God will never leave you or cast you aside? That you will never disgust Him, that He'll never be sorry He chose you? Do you know that?

I hope so. I hope for many of you who have picked up this book that what you're about to read will be a reminder of the freedom you already know you have in Christ—freedom from the penalty of sin, freedom from the tyranny of trying to live up to some impossibly high standard, freedom from the fear of God's displeasure. Freedom from all that and more, and freedom to be who you've been created to be: a child of God, our great King.

*Do you know that if you are His, God will never leave you or cast you aside? That you will never disgust Him, that He'll never be sorry that He chose you? Do you know that?*

And for those who don't even dare to dream about being the girl on the swing, keep reading. I've prayed for you, that God will use my life and His Word to show you how to climb up on your swing. Hey, I'll even give you a push to get you started if you like.

And don't worry if it takes you a while to catch on. God is patient with you. He still smiles whether you know it or not. He grips you securely and won't ever let one of His cherished ones go.

Before I go any further, I have a confession to make. Although I told you that I already know all this, to be honest, I often forget. That's why I write and why I've written this book. I write to remind myself that:

*Neither death nor life, neither angels nor demons,*
*neither the present nor the future, nor any powers, neither*
*height nor depth,*
*nor anything else in all creation,*
*will be able to separate us from the love of God that is in*
*Christ Jesus our Lord.*

ROMANS 8:38–39

And:

*Having loved His own…He loved them to the end.*

JOHN 13:1, NASB

In *Posers, Fakers, and Wannabes*, Brennan Manning writes that the two things that get people's attention are fear and hope. We know about fear, but we're not sure about hope.

> We know about fear,
> but we're not sure about hope.

But our hope is this: When I believe that (a) God is sovereign, that He is all-powerful, all-wise, all-knowing, all-mighty and that He knows exactly what He's doing with the universe and with me, and (b) that, based solely on faith in Christ alone, I am loved completely, totally, utterly—a love that's not conditional on my performance, but on Christ's—when I am convinced of these two things, that's when I find rest and security, hope and freedom.

I find that I have a Father who loves me, a Savior who prays for me, a Comforter who enables me—a God who sets me free.

Once you've learned how to swing, you can't ever unlearn it. Once you've discovered the freedom you already have in Christ, and once you know it, really know it so that it becomes a part of you, you won't ever unknow it.

> *Once you've learned how to swing,*
> *you can't ever unlearn it.*

Likewise, once you've grasped the reality that you live under God's smile…I promise that you will never want to ever live anywhere else.

# Chapter One

# Taking Off My Liar Face

When you're gripped by guilt and shame

*God calls us to stop hiding and come openly to Him. God is the father
who ran to His prodigal son when he came limping home.*
BRENNAN MANNING, *ABBA'S CHILD*

If you and I were to meet, probably the first thing you would
notice about me is my smile. A huge, cheesy grin. It's a bit
crooked, filled with lots of straight teeth, with the exception of
one lower front tooth that's turned slightly. Dental Hygienist Ed
tells me not to ever have it straightened.

My upper gums are receding. Ed says that I brush my teeth
too hard. I try not to, but I forget. I also forget to floss. Sometimes
when Ed is cleaning my teeth, he will shake his head and remind
me that if I want to keep that pretty smile of mine pretty, I need
to floss.

Then, as if on autopilot, even though I'm embarrassed that
I've been caught nonflossing and I'm inwardly berating myself for
knowing better and promising myself and God that from now on

I'll floss every day—and brush more often and more gently—I'll flash Ed a smile so big and bright and winsome and charming that he can't help but think happy, cheery thoughts about me. He might even write on my chart that I've been a good girl, that I work well with others, that I'm cooperative and a pleasure to have in his dental hygienist's chair.

You, Ed, my boss, my husband, my kids, the UPS driver, and the neighbors whose names I don't know, you are all warmed by my smile, won over, at ease. I enter a room smile first. My smile rarely leaves my face. If I were to go on a murderous rampage, after I got caught and the police hauled me into jail, I would smile as they took my mug shot. Eyewitnesses behind the glass would pick me out of the lineup in no time at all.

"That one," they would say. "She did it—the one with the big smile."

The cops would shake their heads in wonder and disbelief. "Who would've thought it could be her," one of them would say. "Behind that smile—a monster."

That's exactly the point. After decades of practice, I've perfected the art of the deceptive smile. Not that I'm consciously aware of it, nor have I sat in front of a mirror and instructed my face what to do. It's just a part of who I am and what I do. It's what I've always done.

I don't remember when I began smiling for nongenuine reasons, not that my smile isn't genuine. I genuinely want you to like me. I genuinely don't want you to know the thoughts I sometimes think and the things I sometimes do.

*After decades of practice, I've perfected the art of the deceptive smile.*

My sister and my youngest brother smile, too. My other brother doesn't, except when he's happy. That would be normal smiling. The rest of us smile when we shouldn't, which is normal for us. For example, if we had done something wrong—let's say we got caught lying—as our mom or dad or teacher scolded us, huge grins would spring onto our faces as if they had minds of their own.

I don't know about my brother or sister, but when that happened to me, I would carry on an internal dialogue with my face.

Me: "Don't do that! You know it makes people crazy. They think you're being a smart aleck. They'll just get madder, and then you'll really be in trouble."

My face: "I know. I know. But I can't help it. If I try not to smile, it'll look like I'm making faces, and that'll be seen as even more smart-alecky. Either way, I'm doomed. At least if I smile, I have a chance of winning them over with my pearly whites."


## Liar, Liar, Face on Fire

When my daughters were little, if I thought they were being deceptive or hiding something, yet no one was squealing, to find out I'd say, "I know you're up to something. You've got your liar face on."

This approach never fails. The guilty one runs to a mirror to look, or she stands still and purses her lips or rubs her cheeks as if to erase the "liar" from her face. Sometimes, out of the blue, a guilty conscience provokes a confession of sorts. Little toddler feet shuffle up, and a sweet voice says, "I'm not wearing my liar face," which means a lie is, indeed, in progress.

*The liar trembles because, above everything else in her life, she desperately wants to be liked.*

Then the little liar smiles, big and bright and toothy, as if a smile could erase all the guilt, all the sin, all the shame of feeling the need to lie in the first place. She smiles because she can't reconcile all the conflicting emotions at the moment, the knowing what needs to come next to be faithful to God, yet the wanting to please and have harmony and to not have to deal with confronting right and wrong—and why can't we just all get along?

The liar trembles because, above everything else in her life, she desperately wants to be liked. She smiles to avoid conflict.

My daughter would smile, too, and no one would be angry at either one of us and everyone would love us forever and ever. After all, isn't that what a smile is for?

## Do These Fig Leaves Come in a Size 8?

At one time people only smiled because they were happy. At one time there was no shame, no guilt, no sin. People didn't have to worry about flossing. They didn't have to worry about approval and acceptance. They didn't have to suppress "bad" feelings like anger. They didn't have to smile so everyone would like them (while not letting anyone know them). They simply smiled.

They simply smiled because they knew the smile of God as they walked with Him in the Garden of Eden. They—the first man, Adam, and his wife, Eve—walked with God and with each other, naked and unashamed (Genesis 2:25).

I don't think it's humanly possible to comprehend being naked—physically, emotionally, spiritually—and unashamed. But at one time, these two people knew no shame, no guilt, no humiliation. They had no need to blush or stammer. They had no secrets to protect, no walking on eggshells with one another, no dancing around hot-button issues. Neither Adam nor Eve had any reason to create liar faces for themselves.

When Eve smiled at Adam, it meant only that she felt 100 percent accepted and cherished by him and by the Lord. Her smile didn't mean, "I hope you'll like me." It didn't mean, "If I smile and look beautiful, I can get you to do what I want."

It didn't mean, "I'm smiling even though I'm angry and afraid of it—afraid that if I tell you what I really think and feel about you, about myself, about this Garden, you'll leave me." Eve smiled because she was naked and unashamed.

> *I don't think it's humanly possible to comprehend being naked—physically, emotionally, spiritually—and unashamed.*

As the story goes, this time of innocence and "unashamed-ness" came to an end when the people did the one thing God had forbidden them to do.

"You are free to eat from any tree in the garden," God had said, "but you must not eat from the tree of the knowledge of good and evil, for when you eat of it you will surely die" (vv. 16–17).

But they ate the fruit anyway, and when they did, it was as God had said. Their eyes were opened to the knowledge of good and evil and all that that knowledge entails. They realized that they were naked, and for the first time they felt what we feel at our nakedness—shame. "So they sewed fig leaves together and made coverings for themselves" (3:7).

Then later, when they heard God's footsteps in the Garden as

He came, as always, for His regular walks with them, the man and his wife hid among the trees.

God called out, "Where are you?"

> *They realized that they were naked, and for the first time they felt what we feel at our nakedness—shame.*

The man answered that he was afraid because he was naked, so he had hidden.

"Who told you that you were naked?" God asked.

That started the first marital blame game. Adam turned to Eve (whom he noticed was smiling a bit too broadly, which was odd, given the seriousness of the moment) and said, "It's your fault, sweetheart."

Next he turned on God. "Actually, it's Your fault, God. You gave her to me."

Eve's smile faded. "Don't blame me," she said. "The snake tricked me."

"Who are you calling a snake?" Adam shot back.

The story continues with God adjudicating them both guilty and proceeding to pass judgment on them: the death penalty. Eventual death of their bodies, immediate death of their souls, and not just for the two of them, but for their children and their children's children—and for us as well.

However, in His great mercy, God also promised them a way that their spirits and ours may live. He promised a Savior, a Redeemer of nakedness and shame. But until then the damage had been done, and we still suffer its effects today.

> *He promised a savior, a Redeemer of nakedness and shame.*

## As Sick As Our Secrets

Kitty Dukakis, wife of former presidential candidate Michael Dukakis, once said in a television interview, "We are as sick as our secrets." Her "secret," which she revealed, was that she was addicted to amphetamines and alcohol. But before she let her secret out, as the wife of a politician she had spent years smiling and pretending all was well when it wasn't.

Back in the early 1990s, researchers James Patterson and Peter Kim surveyed more than two thousand Americans about their most private thoughts and actions, guaranteeing them privacy and anonymity. The results were published in the book *The Day America Told the Truth*.

One of the questions they asked was, "Have you done anything in the previous year for which you feel truly ashamed?" Of the answers, sex, addictions, lies, and stealing topped the list, with sexuality creating the most problems with shameful feelings and thoughts for people. One churchgoing man admitted to having sex with his mother, twice. Another man had had sex with a thirteen-year-old and wanted desperately to undo it. People named incest, abortion, affairs, homosexuality, bestiality, pornography—using it and participating in it.

What was once pure and holy has become perverted by sin, beginning back in the Garden. That's when being naked became shameful. "Most of us (55 percent) hide part of our lives from our closest friends," noted Patterson and Kim. "About the same percentage do things in the privacy of our homes that no one else knows about, that we would never tell anyone.

"We're not even honest with those we say we love," they wrote. "More than two-thirds of us would not confess a one-night stand to our spouses. Most people say that they've hidden their true feelings from a [loved one]. The majority of us would not let our spouses…question us if we were hooked up to a lie detector."

They found that 29 percent—80 million people back then—said that they feel like a "fake, phony, or hypocrite most of the time." They called it a "national facade," millions of people wearing "liar faces."

The truth is, we are naked and we are ashamed.

> *Being naked means being exposed,*
> *and being exposed means that people will see and judge,*
> *and thinking that others are judging brings shame.*

I grew up in California, where the earth shakes without warning. When an earthquake hits, you never know how strong it will be until it's over. I used to be afraid to take showers, afraid that as soon as I took my clothes off and had shampoo in my hair, an earthquake would hit.

Although I was never wild about the idea of my ceiling crashing on my head, truthfully, I was more afraid of rescue workers digging through the rubble that once was my bathroom and finding me naked—and being repulsed. I jokingly called it my "They'll Find Me Nakedaphobia," but it wasn't a joke. It isn't a joke. Being naked means being exposed, and being exposed means that people will see and judge, and thinking that others are judging brings shame.

Shame keeps us awake at night. Like a movie, shame plays in our minds, rewinding and rehashing our most humiliating moments, making sure we won't forget, as if we can forget. Shame has a photographic memory.

Shame sneaks into our thoughts when we're most vulnerable. When we fall in love, it whispers, "You're not good enough. When he finds out the truth about you, he'll run."

When we're up and feeling okay about ourselves, shame kicks

us until we're down; when we're down, it steps on our necks to keep us down. Shame lies so convincingly about who we are that we easily believe it as truth. *Worthless. Ugly. No one will ever love you. If you died, no one would even come to your funeral. That's how insignificant you are.*

Shame keeps us from loving and from receiving love; we're too busy protecting ourselves from further shame. Shame cripples and paralyzes; we cower from it and plead against it. In numerous places in the Bible the psalmist cries out, "Don't let me be put to shame!"

*Shame cripples and paralyzes; we cower from it and plead against it.*

We fear it. We hate it. We run from it, hide from it, lie to cover it. And yet, despite all our best efforts, sometimes we're exposed anyway—and sometimes, instead of finding that it destroys us, we find that it frees us instead.

## Caught in the Act

It was early in the morning. The woman—we don't even know her name—rolled over in the bed that she had shared the night before with a man who was not her husband and ran her finger through his beard. Then, just as he opened his eyes and smiled, the front door creaked open, and before either of them knew what was happening, several of the busiest town busybodies stood at the foot of the bed.

One of the men—these were all teachers of the law, all hotshots—told the man in the bed to get dressed and sneak out the back way. "Next time be more careful," he said, nodding and smiling.

But to the woman he barked, "Get out of that bed!"

The rest of the men all leered at her and laughed as she tried to cover herself with her hands. One held her robe just beyond her reach. Another rooted through her dresser drawers, holding up her clothing for the others to see.

Yet another grabbed her arm and pulled her into the street, still naked. Next, the group of them marched her up to the temple, where Jesus was teaching. They made her stand before the group, and as she shivered in her shame, they broadcast her secret sin: adultery.

> ⸂ *The men leered at her and laughed as she tried to cover herself with her hands.* ⸃

"We caught her in the act," they said. "The law of Moses commands us to stone such women. Now what do you say?" they asked Jesus, trying to trap Him.

But Jesus didn't answer them. Instead, He bent down and started writing in the dirt with His finger. The Bible doesn't say what Jesus wrote, but I like to imagine that He listed some of their own shameful secrets, their own adulteries, lies, corruption.

They kept badgering Jesus with their questions until finally Jesus straightened up and said, "Okay. Go ahead—stone her. Just make sure only those without sin throw first." Then He went back to His writing.

Eventually, everyone walked off until only the woman and Jesus were left. "Where are your accusers?" Jesus asked her. "Does no one condemn you?"

She stood before Him, naked and ashamed, yet at the same time not ashamed. It was as if He saw right through her nakedness to her true self, the one who only dreamed of dancing with innocence like she had done as a child. Back before she felt the need to hide. Back before her life in the darkness and shadows.

"No one, sir," she said.

"Then neither do I condemn you," Jesus told her. "Go now and leave your life of sin" (John 8:1–11, paraphrase mine).

Just as shame was the place where the woman met Jesus, shame is the place where God meets us, too. It's where He loves us deeply, intimately, passionately, unashamedly. His love in the midst of our shame is wild with desire and freeing in its totality.

## "No Raised Eyebrows"

If anyone knows about shame, it's Jim Bakker. Accused of all kinds of shameful, sinful crimes—the image of him in shackles cowering and crying broadcast around the world, his sexual indiscretions making headlines—he was indicted on federal charges of fraud, tax evasion, and racketeering, convicted of fraud and conspiring to commit fraud, and sentenced to forty-five years in federal prison. On top of that, his wife divorced him while he was in prison and then married one of his business associates. We can only imagine the shame and humiliation this man felt.

After his release from prison (he served almost five years), Bakker was interviewed by Steve Brown on his television show, *The Late Steve Brown Show*. When Brown asked him about shame and embarrassment, Bakker smiled.

He admitted that it was difficult and then added, "I'm glad it all happened. Now I can go anywhere and be with anybody in the whole world, and there are no raised eyebrows. I can go into any bar—any social circle of outcasts—and nobody tells me that I ought to be careful because 'people will talk' and that I will 'hurt my reputation.' People have already talked, and I don't have any reputation to hurt. It doesn't matter anymore. I'm free!"

When Bakker discovered that he no longer needed to wear

a liar face, that he was accepted by God solely based on faith in Christ and not on his performance, he also found acceptance by, if not all, at least many of his Christian brothers and sisters.

In 1995, while addressing a Christian leadership conference of ten thousand ministers and clergy, Bakker received a fifteen-minute standing ovation. "I thought people would spit on me," he is quoted as saying. "Instead they received me with open arms."

## My Liar Face Comes Off

As I wrote this, I thought about cataloging all of my own shameful secrets, but frankly, there isn't enough paper to contain them all. But more than that, telling my past secrets isn't necessary because they're gone as far as God is concerned. Listen to what He says:

"Do not be afraid; you will not suffer shame. Do not fear disgrace; you will not be humiliated. You will forget the shame of your youth" (Isaiah 54:4).

"The one who trusts in [Jesus] will never be put to shame" (Romans 9:33).

"Those who look to him are radiant; their faces are never covered with shame" (Psalm 34:5).

"As far as the east is from the west, so far has he removed our transgressions from us" (Psalm 103:12).

> *Telling my past secrets isn't necessary because they're gone as far as God is concerned.*

Sounds good, but…

If you're anything like me, when you're stuck in something—a habit you want to break, a way of thinking that you know is harmful, the replaying of a haunting memory—it's difficult to get unstuck. Habits are notoriously difficult to break.

If worrying were an Olympic event, my daughter Alison would win the gold medal every time. Sometimes when she's up to her eyebrows in nagging what-ifs, I'll tell her, "Just don't worry."

Then she'll slap her forehead and say, "Why didn't I think of that?" As if it's that easy.

Likewise, for someone who is stuck in shameful thoughts of the past, who lives in terror of being found out and exposed, hauled naked into the town square for everyone to see and judge, having someone say, "Just stop being ashamed," is mostly meaningless. It either makes you more ashamed for not being able to control your thoughts—or you want to smack the person for being glib.

> *For someone who is stuck in shameful thoughts of the past, having someone say, "Just stop being ashamed," is mostly meaningless.*

My friend Steve, whom I often refer to as my "uncle-dad," is among other things a pastor and a Bible teacher. He's also quite wise and gives great counsel. He once told me that, although it's not possible to be 100 percent unashamed this side of heaven, because of Jesus, those who operate out of shame can experience moments of freedom.

That's all life is—moments. So for those who are ashamed, in those moments, consider Jesus. All the sins that He wrote in the dirt, all of my sins, all of yours, all of our combined guilt and shame, all the memories that we carry and can't erase from our consciences, all the nakedness and the feelings of embarrassment, humiliation, and worthlessness—all of that Jesus took as His own.

He who had never had a lustful thought became lust. He who had never stolen a candy bar, never punched His little brother, never sassed or disappointed His mother, never lied—He became sin in our place. He allowed Himself to be humiliated, shamed, beaten, spat on, hung naked upon a cross, crucified.

In our moments of shame, Jesus calls us to consider Him upon the cross.

*When I consider Him, consider His pardon, and consider that my sinful soul He counts as free, I smile.*

A verse from the hymn "Before the Throne," written by Charitie L. Bancroft in 1863, goes:

When Satan tempts me to despair, and tells me of the guilt within, upward I look and see Him there, who made an end to all my sin. Because the sinless Savior died, my sinful soul is counted free. For God the just is satisfied, to look on Him and pardon me.

In moments of shame, when my mind replays those old mental video clips and I'm haunted by memories of things I now regret, "upward I look and see Him there" and tell myself that "God the just is satisfied" and that, because of Jesus, "there is now no condemnation for those who are in Christ Jesus" (Romans 8:1).

In those moments, when I consider Him, consider His pardon, and consider that in all my moments my sinful soul He counts as free, I smile. Not the liar face smile that hides my secret self, but the smile of the Garden. The smile of someone who, if only for a moment, tastes the sweetness of being naked and unashamed.

# Think on These Things

*Think:* What are some of the more obvious types of false fronts, masks, or facades ("liar faces") that people use in our society? What are some more subtle ways that people hide their true selves? Why do you think people feel the need to hide?

*Study:* Using a dictionary and a thesaurus, do a word study on *guilt* and *shame*. What is the difference between the two words? What is "false" guilt? Now discover what the Bible says about the words. Using an index or a concordance, look up each word and find the Bible passage that corresponds to each entry. To get you started, here are some Scripture references about shame: Psalm 34:5; Isaiah 54:4–5; and Isaiah 61:7.

*Apply:* Throughout the Bible, God invites, even commands, His children to come to Him with their every need, including haunting, condemning thoughts. Look up 1 John 3:19–20 and 2 Corinthians 10:5, Scripture passages that deal with how and what we think. How can you use these Scriptures to combat shameful, invading thoughts?

*Consider:* Hebrews 10:22–23 says, "Let us draw near to God with a sincere heart in full assurance of faith, having our hearts sprinkled to cleanse us from a guilty conscience and having our bodies washed with pure water. Let us hold unswervingly to the hope we profess, for he who promised is faithful." How would your life be different if you truly believed this?

*Meditate:* "If we conceal our wounds out of fear and shame, our inner darkness can neither be illuminated nor become a light for others." —Brennan Manning, *Abba's Child*

# Chapter Two

# Deeply Flawed, Dearly Loved

### When you doubt God's acceptance of you

God *is for us. God* is *for us. God is* for *us. God is for* us.
MAX LUCADO, *IN THE GRIP OF GRACE*

I don't love God.

Does that shock you? It shocks me to say it, to see it in black and white and make it public.

*I don't love God.*

At least not the way I'd like to or the way that I think I should. I think that I should always think about Him and not make any decisions without first consulting Him in prayer. I think that everything that I do should be to honor Him and give Him glory. I'd like it to, but I know it doesn't.

If I loved God, I'd keep His commandments. That's what Jesus told His disciples. He said, "If you love me, keep my commandments." But I don't keep them. If I try real hard, outwardly I could probably appear to keep maybe three or four of the Top Ten, but inwardly, in my heart and mind and motives, I don't think I could keep even one. If I loved God, you would think I could keep at least one!

I don't think I love God. Here's an example of why I think that. Several months ago I was scheduled to speak to a group of women at a one-day retreat. I had planned to speak about the things that hold us captive and keep us from experiencing the smile of God on our lives. I had spoken on that topic dozens of times before, so knowledge of the subject matter wasn't the problem. The problem was that my mind was on other things, and not even worthy things like America being at war or people starving in Ethiopia. That would be understandable, even forgivable. But I hadn't been thinking about those things or even about the women I was going to be with.

Instead, a week prior to the retreat, when I should have been deep in prayer and study and meditation, I was glued to my chair at my computer, searching the Internet for bed linens. Not just any bed linens—the "perfect" bed linens.

I kept telling myself, "Think retreat. Think retreat." But thoughts of pillow shams and blankets kept interrupting. That made me feel guilty, which made me hop in the car and head for the mall, where I bought a wrought iron headboard, a bed skirt, a blanket, a coverlet, a set of crisp white sheets, two additional sets of pillowcases, and a purple throw pillow. I didn't think I could live without the purple pillow.

It gets worse. Just as I thought that that should surely satisfy my lust for linens, I started thinking about the next time I would change my bedroom, as if I needed both summer linens *and* winter linens. Thinking about that made me think that I needed to do some extra praying or do something super religious to keep God from shaking His head in disgust and flicking me in the back of my head with His cosmic finger. But how much praying is enough? Besides, wouldn't God see that my motives weren't pure and, therefore, cancel out any religious stuff I might do? If you ask me, it's all quite pathetic, which is exactly why I think that I don't love God.

There's more. Jesus also said that people will know His followers by the way they love one another. I'm not good at loving the "anothers" in my life—I'm usually too busy loving myself. If I don't even love one "another," and if loving one another is evidence of loving God, then I'm afraid I don't love God.

I'm afraid. I don't love God, and that makes me afraid.

Once I met a woman who sings for Jesus. "I love the Lord so much! I just want to honor Him with the talent He's given me," she said. That made me feel slimy. Not about her but about me. I also want to honor God with the talent He's given me, but sometimes that's almost a second or third thought. My first thought is usually about earning a paycheck with my talent. My second thought is about buying wheat-colored pillow shams.

*I'm not good at loving the "anothers" in my life—*
*I'm usually too busy loving myself.*

I don't think I love God.

If I loved God, I would love His Word—all of it. Once at church I signed up to read the entire Bible in a year, but I got stuck at Leviticus. I told my pastor, "Leviticus is boring." So I skipped over it. Does that mean I don't love God? If I loved God, wouldn't I love Leviticus as much as I do the Psalms or Ephesians?

I love the things God does for me. I love the peace He gives in the storms of life and the joy He gives, even in sorrow. I love the family He has given me. I love His gifts. I love sunsets and oak trees and sourdough bread. I love His mercy and grace and His patience with me in my foolishness. But I'm not sure if I love Him. What if He took away everything I love—would I love

Him? I don't know, and that bothers me. What if, because I don't love God, He decides to not love me? That's the real issue. How do I know that God loves me?

## Bumper Sticker Love

According to the bumper sticker on my car, I enjoy God. That's the "chief end of man," as written in the Westminster Shorter Catechism—"The chief end of man is to glorify God and to enjoy Him forever." However, is enjoying God and loving God the same thing? I don't think you can love God without enjoying Him, but what about enjoying Him without loving Him? Is that possible?

*According to the bumper sticker on my car, I enjoy God.*

Recently, I sent an e-mail to the one I call my uncle-dad, who knows about these things, mostly because he wrestles with the same kinds of questions. He said that when he learned the "enjoying God" catechism, he set out to enjoy Him with all his might, thinking that the more he worked at it, the more he would enjoy Him and the more he would glorify Him. But the opposite happened. The harder he worked at enjoying God, the less he actually enjoyed Him.

Eventually, he gave up and went out for a movie and an ice-cream cone. "Then I started feeling guilty," he said. "I decided that I was a worm, and after all that Jesus had done for me, I ought to enjoy Him more. What kind of Christian was I anyway if I enjoyed a movie and an ice-cream cone more than God?"

But then he discovered that when he went to the movie, God didn't turn His back on him or flick him in the back of his head. "So I went to the movie, and here is the important and surprising thing: God went to the movie with me! In fact, He was everywhere I was and wouldn't let me alone…He pursued me gently, kindly, and graciously. [He] never demanded that I love Him or enjoy Him the way He loved me and, it had become apparent, He enjoyed being with me."

My uncle-dad concluded, "Just let God love you and the time will come when—almost without knowing it—you will find that you love Him back and, not only that, you enjoy hanging out with Him."

Ever the skeptic, I e-mailed him back and told him that, in theory, I liked his answer, but in practice, I still wasn't sure.

> ↶ *"Just let God love you and the time will come when you find that you love Him back and, not only that, you enjoy hanging out with Him."* ↷

He e-mailed back and asked: "Why do you think you *need* to love God? Do you think His love for you is somehow based on your love for Him? What if it's true—that you don't love Him? Will that keep Him from loving you? What you're really asking is, 'What criteria does God use in His decision to love a person?' You think about it, then get back to me."

## The Gospel According to Tara

As I thought about it, I remembered that the early church wrestled with some of the same questions. In the province of Galatia, the apostle Paul had come to them with a radical message from God: There's nothing—no sacrifice, no offering, no good deed, no effort, no ceremony or ritual—nothing a person can do to obtain God's favor. It's Jesus and Jesus alone.

At one time Paul had been a strict student and keeper of God's law, until he met Jesus face-to-face and realized that it is by grace alone that a person is made right with God. It's a gift, and you don't pay back a gift or it isn't a gift to begin with. To do so would be an affront to the Gift Giver. "For it is by grace you have been saved, through faith—and this not from yourselves, it is the gift of God—not by works, so that no one can boast" (Ephesians 2:8–9). That was the message that Paul took to all the churches that he visited and the message that God's churches are built on today.

However, it's human nature to want to do life apart from God, to do something, anything. My pastor says that's the essence of sin. Not that we do bad things, although that's the result of the sin that's already going on in our insides. But the essence of sin is to look on Jesus and the message of grace alone by faith alone and say, "That's nice, Lord, but let's add this and that to it."

> *It's human nature to want to do life apart from God, to do something, anything.*

For the Galatians, that meant that to be accepted by God, one must believe Christ died to pay the penalty of sin, and, just in case that wasn't enough, let's add circumcision. For us in the twenty-first century, since we view circumcision as a medical procedure performed on baby boys, we have a whole menu of options to add to our faith. Faith in Christ is the standard model; things like faithful church attendance and regular Bible study and prayer are the upgrades.

I'm not saying these are bad things—they are good, even necessary things. But they are not the basis of God's acceptance of us. It's either Jesus plus nothing or it's nothing. Pass or fail. In or out.

In his letter to the Galatian church, Paul wrote adamantly, even furiously. He said, "I can't believe your fickleness—how easily you have turned traitor to him who called you" (Galatians 1:6, *The Message*). In another place he said, "We know very well that we are not set right with God by rule-keeping but only through personal faith in Jesus Christ" (2:16, *The Message*). He told them that he had tried it the other way, "working my head off to please God, and it didn't work. So I quit being a 'law man' so that I could be *God's* man" (v. 19, *The Message*).

He went on to call them crazy, foolish, "dear idiots" and accused them of having a hex or spell put on them (depending on which Bible translation you're looking at). He asked them, "How did your new life begin? Was it by working your heads off to please God? Or was it by responding to God's Message to you? Are you going to continue this craziness? For only crazy people would think they could complete by their own efforts what was begun by God. If you weren't smart enough or strong enough to begin it, how do you suppose you could perfect it?" (3:2–4, *The Message*).

> *It's either Jesus plus nothing or it's nothing. Pass or fail. In or out.*

Next he presented them with the core of the gospel of grace. He asked, "Does the God who lavishly provides you with his own presence, his Holy Spirit, working things in your lives you could never do for yourselves, does he do these things because of your strenuous moral striving *or* because you trust him to do them in you?" (3:5–6, *The Message*).

Then he added, "Doing things for God is the opposite of entering into what God does for you" (3:11, *The Message*).

Or as my friend Tara says, "We stink—God rules." That's the bare-bones gospel, plain and simple.

## Confessions of a Crazy Galatian

So I sent another e-mail to my uncle-dad and told him that if I understand the Bible correctly, God loves me simply and solely because He does. He's not impressed that I sit in the front row at church and take notes or that I once read the entire book of Ephesians in the waiting room at the car dealership while I waited to get my oil changed (and that I didn't watch *The Price Is Right* like everyone else there did).

He loves me just because He does, and He accepts me simply and solely based on my faith in Christ—and that isn't even of my doing. Even my faith is a gift from Him.

I stink—God rules.

> As my friend Tara says, "We stink—God rules."
> That's the bare-bones gospel, plain and simple.

My pastor likes to use the word *impute*. We have *imputed* righteousness. Jesus says, "Okay, since you've already blown any chance of being good enough for My Father's kingdom, if you trust Me, I'll give you My perfect record. Plus, I've already taken the death penalty in your place. So, I'll trade you your sin-filled life for My sinless one. That way, when the Father looks at you, He'll see Me, and He will accept you because He accepts Me. Remember, trust Me on this one."

By faith, Christ imputes His righteousness to my account.

❧

In his next e-mail, my uncle-dad said, "You get a gold star for having right doctrine, but you still need some work on your real-life believing it; for example, your wondering about whether or not you love God. When you wonder if you love God, you're really wondering if God loves you. So here's what I want you to do. I want you to take your daughter shopping. We'll talk later."

*⟲ You need to know that my relationship with Laura has been, at times, complicated. ⟳*

Since I had been planning a trip to North Carolina to visit my daughter Laura, this assignment was well timed, albeit a bit odd.

You need to know that my relationship with Laura has been, at times, complicated. We love each other dearly, but we've struggled. I apologize if I seem vague; I'm not at liberty to confess her sins, only mine, and I plan on confessing many in the following pages, so keep reading.

Let's just say that, since she was in high school, she has been prone to wander. But then, aren't we all? Some just do it outwardly and with more noise and flair than others.

When I got to Charlotte, Laura picked me up at the airport and we made a plan: We would eat ourselves stupid and shop ourselves senseless. It's always good to have attainable goals.

Now, I've shopped with Laura hundreds of times. When she lived at home, we would go to the outlet stores and come back with more stuff than we needed or even wanted, some of which we never wore. After a few months, we would clean out our closets and bring the clothes, often with the tags still on, to the Goodwill store and go out for more. When you have no need, things mean nothing.

This shopping trip was different, however. I had told her to make a list of what she really, really wanted. I've seen her lists before, but not like this one. For a year she had been living on ramen noodles and dollar tacos, and with great thought she wrote feverishly, putting her deepest wishes down on paper. Then as we wheeled a shopping cart up and down the aisles of Target, I watched as her dreams came true: laundry soap and shampoo, packages of pens, rolls of tape.

"Can I have some bleach—and fabric softener, too?" she asked at one point. A far cry from the "Mom, I need a new CD!" of years before. When you're aware of your need, anything means everything.

And because I love her just because she's mine, I loved buying her bleach and Lysol and throw pillows for her couch and candles for her bathroom counter, a picture for her bare living room wall, a pair of pink jeans. Later, as we lugged the shopping bags up the three flights of stairs to her apartment and she oohed and aahed over the jars of peanut butter and cartons of yogurt and cans of tuna, my heart beat fast and I tossed my head back and laughed. I thought, *I bet this is a taste of the delight God feels when He gives His kids gifts.*

> *Because I love her just because she's mine, I loved buying her bleach and Lysol and throw pillows for her couch and candles for her bathroom counter, a picture for her bare living room wall, a pair of pink jeans.*

I also realized that my daughter "gets" the concept of grace. She thanked me repeatedly, but not excessively or neurotically. She said, "At this stage in my life right now I have nothing, so all I can say is thank you."

And because she knew that none of my gifts came with strings attached, she didn't feel guilty or as if she needed to repay me or do something to "prove" her love. She had sent me a card a year earlier in which she wrote, "I know at times I have acted ungrateful, but I have always appreciated you. I also know that I have been difficult at times and flat-out bad. It means the world to me that you have always stuck by me…you are the best mom in the entire world, and one day I hope to be like you. I love you more than anyone in the entire world."

You would have to know our history to fully comprehend the depth of meaning behind her words. Our joke between us is that one day she, a now-toned-down goth-punk-bohemian, will stand up in church wearing a "come to Jesus" dress and testify. Right now, however, she's still gathering material for her testimony. That's all I'm going to say about that; you can draw your own conclusions.

On the way back to Florida I thought about my daughter, both of my daughters, and also about God and how His gifts of mercy and grace come without strings attached. Laura had said, "I have nothing; all I can do is say thanks," and then she went and stacked her cans of tuna with the delight of a child on Christmas morning playing with her toys.

Only those who recognize their need can truly appreciate a gift.

*On the way back to Florida I thought about my daughters, and also about God and how His gifts of mercy and grace come without strings attached.*

I left there knowing that when I got back to Florida, the chances were great that the next time Laura and I talked, one of us would tick the other one off and we might have a cold war for a few days, but that I would never—I could never—tell her that she was no longer my daughter. I might not approve or agree with a lot of the decisions she makes or the things she does, but I always, always, always accept her as my own. Even if she were to turn her back on me, she will always be mine. *I love her simply because she's mine.*

# When God Sings

I don't know the name of the song, but it's sung by Vanessa Williams, and years ago whenever it would come on the radio, Laura and I would call out, "That's Vanessa Williams!" Well, on the way home from the Tampa airport after my visit with Laura, that song played on my car radio and, as I had always done, I called out, "That's Vanessa Williams!" and sang along. I can't explain it except to say, it was like it became a hymn. Not that the words of the song were sacred, or even about God, but it was as if God were singing it through me to my kid five hundred miles away—singing to the one who used to make me so crazy, the one I would wait up for until 3 or 4 a.m. The one for whom I would scream my prayers to God.

It was strange and holy and silly all at the same time, singing this song, alone in my car.

Then God sang. Not really, but really.

> *It was strange and holy and silly all at the same time, singing this song, alone in my car.*

The prophet Zephaniah wrote:

> Sing, O Daughter of Zion; shout aloud, O Israel! Be glad and rejoice with all your heart, O Daughter of Jerusalem! The Lord has taken away your punishment, he has turned back your enemy. The Lord, the King of Israel, is with you; never again will you fear any harm.… The Lord your God is with you, he is mighty to save. He will take great delight in you, he will quiet you with his love, he will rejoice over you with singing. (Zephaniah 3:14–15, 17)

In my car God sang of His love for me—the one who doesn't love Him as I should or even as I want to. He sang because He sang. He sang because I trust in His Son. He sang because, even though I get things wrong most of the time and right only some of the time, I'm His anyway and nothing will change that as far as He's concerned. He has taken away my punishment, and that's why He sings. He sings because of Jesus, and so do I.

*I am, in God's eyes, deeply flawed yet dearly loved, and it doesn't make sense, but oh, well.*

When I got home, I e-mailed my uncle-dad and told him about buying Laura bleach and fabric softener and about Vanessa Williams on the radio and hearing God sing. I told him that I think I understand stuff better, maybe not completely, but enough not to drive myself batty worrying if I need to do something for God (and worrying even more that sometimes I don't want to do anything for Him).

I told him that I had come to the conclusion that I am, in God's eyes, at the same time deeply flawed, yet dearly loved, and that it doesn't make sense, but oh, well. Loving your kid doesn't make sense sometimes either.

He e-mailed me back and told me to eat an ice-cream cone. So I did.

# Think on These Things

*Think:* Some people think it sounds arrogant to claim "God loves me." Why might they believe that? What makes a person lovable to God?

*Study:* At the time of the Reformation, church reformers proclaimed the doctrine of "faith alone." Martin Luther, a German monk, spent much of his early life agonizing over his sin and his desire to be made right with God, to the point of raging at God because of his tormented soul.

Read Romans 1:16–17, the passage that became Luther's epiphany, when he "got" the gospel and the concept of grace. Using a concordance, look up other Scriptures about faith. What do you conclude about what the Bible means by "The righteous will live by faith"?

*Apply:* For those who struggle with believing that they are forever accepted by the Father because of their faith in Christ, how would the following Scriptures be of encouragement? John 6:37–40; 10:27–30; Romans 8:38–39; Galatians 2:16; Hebrews 13:5.

Compare these Scriptures to the role of good works in a Christian's life in the following passages: Philippians 2:12–13; Colossians 1:10; James 2:17; 1 Peter 2:12. How are faith and deeds interrelated?

*Consider:* What does it mean to you to know that God sings over you? (See Zephaniah 3:17.) If you truly believed that, how would your everyday life be different?

*Meditate:* "The central reality for Christians is the personal, unalterable, persevering commitment God makes to us. Perseverance is not the result of our determination, it is the result of God's faithfulness. We survive in the way of faith not because we have extraordinary stamina but because God is righteous, because God sticks with us." —Eugene Peterson, *God's Message for Each Day*

# Chapter Three

# Eternal Umbilicus

### When you're controlled by fear

*Mom, I'm not twelve years old.*
LAURA KENNEDY, AGE 22

I'm having trouble with my neighbor lady. You see, I have a daughter whom I'm trying to raise as best I can, but this neighbor lady keeps interfering.

She's nice and all, and I know she means well, but she makes my job as a parent a living nightmare. For example, I don't want my daughter to have everything handed to her. I think that struggle is good and necessary, even vital, for strong character development. Think of a certain blond, vapid, morally deficient socialite who's always in the tabloids—that's exactly who I don't want my daughter to become.

But this neighbor lady! Every time it looks like my daughter might not have the newest hot thing, this neighbor lady rushes right out and gets it and appears on our doorstep, bearing bags and boxes of gifts. She's constantly throwing money at my kid—heaven forbid my daughter has to save her money for something she wants or go without.

She's always undoing everything that I, as my daughter's parent, am trying to do, and she constantly gets in the way of what I'm trying to accomplish. When I correct my kid, she jumps right in between us and uncorrects it, as if she's somehow protecting my own kid from me, her own parent! This woman has some nerve.

Here's another example of how this neighbor lady makes me nuts. Let's say I want to teach my daughter how to ride a bike. We'll go out on the trail by our house where it's perfectly safe, and as soon as my daughter starts to pedal and it looks like she's wobbling a bit and might fall, this neighbor lady, who will be lurking in the bushes watching us—I mean, doesn't this woman have a life?—will run out and grab on to my daughter's bike, which will throw her off balance, and she'll end up running into a tree. In the end, all the neighbor lady's good intentions actually hurt my kid, which is the opposite of what she wants to happen, but that's what happens.

*Sometimes I think there's no hope in this situation.
I may have to kill her, which is a problem.*

Sometimes I hate this neighbor lady, and I've screamed at her repeatedly to LEAVE MY KID ALONE! She'll go away for a little while, but she always comes back with new and improved ways to make a mess of things. She's ruining my life, and I'm at my wit's end as to what to do about her. Sometimes I think there's no hope in this situation. I may have to kill her, which is a problem.

I just told you a story that God recently told me. The punch line is: He is the parent in the story, and I'm the neighbor lady. Ouch.

# A Tale of Two Daughters and
# Their Lunatic Mother

I have two daughters. Alison, my firstborn, is grown and married to a good man and is the mother of my granddaughter, Caroline Kennedy Smith. All of her life, Alison mostly did all the right things, at least outwardly, and I've never worried about her. She's cautious and careful. She's delightful and funny and a great cook. Now that she's a wife and mother, we've become friends. She refreshes me, makes me laugh. I am infinitely proud of Alison, and at least on my part, there's no struggle between us.

And then there's Laura.

Laura is…edgy. When Laura was in high school, she and her group of equally edgy friends would sit out on the dock and smoke smelly cigars. (At the time, that's all I was aware of that they were smoking.) Laura is the type of person you either love or hate. She's in your face, impulsive. When she was seventeen, she campaigned nonstop for a tattoo and eyebrow piercings. We compromised by having her nose pierced.

Her peer group at church called themselves the Sunday school slackers. She's been goth, punk, and grunge. Today she describes herself as "punk-bohemian-Rhoda Morgenstern from *The Mary Tyler Moore Show*." She's definitely out there.

When she was twenty and going nowhere with her life, she left Florida for North Carolina, an answer to her prayer. One day she told me, "Mom, I don't make a habit of this, but I prayed. I said, 'Dear God, get me out of this place!'"

Almost immediately, a girl she had known in high school called. Julie had moved to Charlotte, North Carolina, and needed a roommate and thought maybe Laura would want to drop everything and move in with her.

It sounded just crazy enough for Laura to say yes. "Do you

think this is God's answer?" she asked. I told her to ask her dad. The joke in our family is that my husband is notorious for not liking any idea that isn't his. But he loved this idea and even offered to help move Laura up there. So, with a few thousand dollars that she had saved and an address to an apartment that she had never seen in a city that she had never been to, she left home to start a new life. A fresh start with fresh hope and endless possibilities.

It would be wonderful, and everyone (especially me) would live happily ever after.

I had it all planned. After a day or two of getting settled in, Laura would go out early on Monday morning and pound the pavement, looking for a job. Because I wanted her to be of strong character, my plan was to not have her get the first job she applied for, but maybe the second or third.

> *It would be wonderful, and everyone (especially me) would live happily ever after.*

Not as planned, she wrecked her car her first day there. Next, she got sick. Then someone in her apartment building left bleach residue in the washing machine, which ruined her load of black clothes. Her bed didn't arrive for a week, so she had to sleep on the floor, which smelled like cat urine. It rained every day and she cried, also every day. She would call home and tell me how much she hated it and wanted to come home.

For two weeks she applied for every job she could, but no one hired her. She began to panic as she watched her bank account dwindle. A dream date turned out to be a dud.

The last straw, for me anyway, came when she learned that her car wouldn't be ready when the repair shop people had said it would be. She had been driving my husband's truck while her car was in the shop, but he had already flown up to Charlotte and had driven it home and she was stuck with an important job interview to go to and no way to get there.

It took the full resurrection force of the Holy Spirit to keep me from telling her, "I'll be right there." I would just drive the five hundred miles and take her myself to the job interview. After all, God obviously wasn't doing His job taking care of my kid, and if He was just going to sit on His hands and not help her, then I would.

I was in full neighbor lady mode as I thought, *This isn't the first time God didn't do His job*. Like, where was He when she crashed her car in the first place? Like, despite the fact that I had blitzed the Charlotte area by writing letters to women's ministry leaders at churches that I thought Laura should go to, introducing myself and telling them about Laura (adding, "By the way, if you see her, please take care of her for me since I'm so far away." I even sent along copies of my books and hinted that I speak at retreats, hoping to maybe get an invitation or two and thus get a free trip to see my kid)—despite all that, didn't God realize that she only knew one other person in Charlotte, who had to work and couldn't drive Laura to her job interview? Hello?! How was she going to get there?

> *It took the full resurrection force of the Holy Spirit to keep me from telling her, "I'll be right there."*

Obviously, God didn't realize that this wasn't supposed to happen. My plan, which I had thought was God's plan, didn't have any provision for her being miserable and hopeless. Maybe a bit challenged, but not like this.

So, I was ticked at God for not taking care of my kid. I was ticked because I couldn't zip on up to North Carolina and fix things for her, ticked because I missed her. I was ticked because I thought I could do God's job better than He could and ticked because He wouldn't step aside so I could prove it to Him.

I was so ticked that I skipped church and went to the movies. I saw *Bruce Almighty*.

The main character, Bruce, takes God on. As Bruce sees the situation, he's an ant and God is a mean kid sitting on a hill with a magnifying glass burning Bruce's feelers off. Bruce doesn't think God is good at running the universe, at least his section of it, and so God steps aside and gives Bruce the chance to be almighty. Of course, Bruce gets overwhelmed with the job, especially when it comes to answering the prayers of millions of people. His solution is a blanket "yes" across the board, which causes chaos.

Not that I wanted to be Nancy Almighty in the universal sense, just N.A. in Laura's life, at least until she found herself a secure job with a steady income, a good man to marry, a generous retirement plan, and adequate health insurance. Is that too much to ask?

The problem is, God wants to be (and is) almighty, and He makes my attempts at being it downright difficult. In our wrestling matches, I would say He wins ten times out of ten, and I end up in a heap on the floor.

Remind me to tell you later what happened with Laura's car and the job interview.


## Eternal Umbilicus

I had come to the re-conclusion that I hated trusting God. (I say "re" because I keep coming back to this one thing, like the proverb that says, "As a dog returns to its vomit, so a fool repeats his folly.") I hated trusting God with the full force of my mind, body, and soul, especially when it came to my kid. *Trust is too difficult, too scary*, I thought. Even now I'm still not crazy about it, but I'm getting better.

*Not that I wanted to be Nancy Almighty in the universal sense, just N.A. in Laura's life, at least until she found herself a secure job with a steady income, a good man to marry, a generous retirement plan, and adequate health insurance. Is that too much to ask?*

So, as I fretted and stewed and tried to be Nancy Almighty, I stumbled upon a *Psychology Today* article titled "A Nation of Wimps," which detailed the ludicrous things that parents do to take the bumps out of life for their children. What they think is good parenting is, in reality, producing young adults who don't know how to solve their own problems (or turn to God for help).

It used the term "eternal umbilicus," referring to cell phones, those almost-magical devices lunatic moms like me carry around at all times just in case their precious beloveds stub their toes and need Mommy to make it all better. I don't leave home without it.

Not only do I have my cell phone by my side at all times, but I've also discovered AOL Instant Messaging and that moms can check their Buddy List to see how long their child has been away from the computer. So, for example, if I happened to get up at 3 a.m. and check my Buddy List and notice that Laura hadn't been at her computer for, say, ten hours, and if I happened to jump to the conclusion that she must be out doing God knows what, I could then whip out my cell phone and give her a call "just to say hi."

*I came to the re-conclusion that I hated trusting God. (I say "re" because I keep coming back to this one thing, like the proverb that says, "As a dog returns to its vomit, so a fool repeats his folly.")*

Thanks to technology, I can be an even greater lunatic long distance than I ever was when she lived in the same house. When she first moved to North Carolina, I would search the online want ads, and I even made an appointment with an employment counselor for her. Daily, I checked the weather report for Charlotte to make sure that it wasn't going to snow or be icy. And as long as I could stay connected to her via cell phone and Instant Messaging, I could function. That eternal umbilicus thing.

Then disaster struck. Her Internet went down and so did her cell phone—at the same time. I didn't hear from her for what seemed like weeks. Without my regular and constant input, I imagined her destitute and covered with boils, beaten up in an alley, begging for soup from rich socialite ladies. Or she was in a hospital with amnesia, or depressed on her couch, unable to get up.

That's when I started to consider that maybe I had a problem. A "control issue," as they say. Recently, I met a woman who called herself Ms. Control Freak, and I had to laugh. "Oh, Honey," I told her, "you're a lightweight." I told her about all the things I've done to "help" Laura—like driving forty miles one-way to the nearest branch of Laura's bank to make deposits in her account so she would never have to deal with the consequences of having a check bounce. I did that not once, but many times. One day the bank lady looked me in the eye and said, "Don't do it, Mom." How did she know?

Anyway, Ms. Control Freak conceded the title to me. Like I said, lightweight.

Back to the *Psychology Today* article. Even before I read it, even before God told me the story of the neighbor lady, I knew I had a problem. It's like alcoholics know they're alcoholics, drug addicts know they're addicts, even if they won't admit it. I was a Laura addict and needed to find the nearest Umbilicus Anonymous meeting. But since there aren't any in my area, I went to see my friend Tara instead.

## The Story of the Prodigal Mom

Before I tell you about my visit with Tara, let me finish the story about Laura's car, her job interview, and what I got from the *Bruce Almighty* movie, beginning with the movie.

By the ending credits, God remained God and all was well. Although the movie's theology wasn't biblically accurate, I loved Morgan Freeman as God, who remained calm and good-natured throughout Bruce's rantings. He wasn't intimidated, didn't retaliate or smite Bruce with boils or locusts. He never lost His cool. Instead, God's demeanor toward Bruce was like that of a loving Father, patiently watching His headstrong toddler struggling to put his pants on upside down, yet refusing to admit he can't do it. With genuine affection, the Father just smiles and waits.

I laughed throughout the movie, but I cried on the way home. How like God to deliver His message, "Be still, and know that I am God" (Psalm 46:10), in such a gracious manner. So I repented of my own rantings against Him concerning His care of my daughter.

> God's demeanor toward Bruce was like that of a loving Father, patiently watching his headstrong toddler struggling to put his pants on upside down, yet refusing to admit he can't do it.

But…she still needed to get to her job interview on Monday.

When I got home from the movies, I discovered a message on my answering machine. Laura had called to say she found a ride. The next day she called to say that out of ninety-five applicants, she got the job. Later that day she got her car back. All was well, roll the movie credits.

Except…

I forget so easily. When Laura is doing well, when I see God's hand in her life, then I am at peace. But the minute she runs into difficulty or tells me about a plan to do something that would require me to keep my mouth shut and trust God, which by now you know I would rather eat cut glass than do, that neighbor lady leaps into action.

The morning I went to see Tara, Laura had e-mailed me to say that she and her roommate were driving to Atlanta for a concert. In my opinion, no one should ever drive to Atlanta because the traffic is nuts, and at the time I didn't think Laura had enough driving experience to handle big-city traffic. So, I fired off a fear-laden sermonette on the perils of the road and the virtues of staying home and not putting herself in danger, blah, blah, blah.

"Do you have a plan?" I wrote. "Have you thought about what you would do if you got into an accident?" As soon as I pressed Send, I immediately regretted it. She replied that she's not twelve years old anymore and didn't appreciate me treating her like she was. She told me to mind my own business and to let her make her own mistakes. "Otherwise, how will I learn?" she asked. The problem is, I still see her as a twelve-year-old and feel the need to guide her every step. I still think her business is my business.

*something happens when friends meet to pray. God shows up and convicts of sin and melts hard hearts.*

When I met with Tara, I knew I needed to pray. I told her how much I hated trusting God with Laura and about how angry I had made her (and rightly so). I told her that I felt like "breaking up" with Laura—never talk to her ever again and won't she be sorry she was mean to me. If she could be a baby, then I'd just be a bigger one. So there.

But something happens when friends meet to pray. God shows up and convicts of sin and melts hard hearts. As we prayed and talked, Tara reminded me of the story of the runaway Prodigal Son that Jesus told His followers in Luke 15. In the story, a father has two sons. The youngest wants to leave his father's house and go wild, so he in essence tells his dad, "I wish you were dead; let me have my inheritance and I'm outa here."

The son leaves for a "far country," squanders his money on booze and prostitutes, then ends up eating garbage and sleeping in alleyways. Eventually he longs to return home and does so. Although he expects to have to beg his father's forgiveness and his highest hope is to become a servant, when the father sees his son's frame off in the distance, he runs full bore to meet him. The father is ecstatic that his son has returned and throws a great party to celebrate. The father and the son are reunited, and they live happily ever after.

Tara said, "What if the father in the story hadn't let the boy go? The son might never have come to the end of himself and returned fully repentant."

Although Laura's leaving home was under much different circumstances (she didn't leave home in anger or defiant rebellion like the boy in the story), in her own way she's off in a "far country."

Later that day, I received a well-timed e-mail devotion that said, "Overprotective parents do their children a great injustice." I knew that, but I needed to know it again. I know that it's struggle and hardship that form our character and serve to create an awareness of our need for God. Plus, if we never have a need to trust Him, how will we know that God is trustworthy? The most loving thing I can do for my child is to let her make her own mistakes and learn from them, just as the father in the story let his son go.

The devotional went on to describe how the Israelites were led by God out of Egypt only to be pursued by the Egyptian army until they were penned in at the shore of the Red Sea. With certain death before and behind them, the Israelites accused God of playing a cruel joke on them.

Then the Red Sea parted. The Israelites escaped, and all the pursuing Egyptians drowned. "God puts us against the 'Red Seas' in order to show His power in and through us," wrote the devotional writer. "If we do not know God can deliver, then we can never learn to trust Him. Circumstances that go beyond our capabilities of solving them place us at God's complete mercy."

Thankfully, God is completely merciful to His children, which includes my daughter as well as me. As a repentant prodigal, once I returned to my Father to ask His forgiveness, I called Laura, who was already on her way to Atlanta, to ask her forgiveness, too.

> "If we do not know God can deliver,
> then we can never learn to trust Him.
> Circumstances that go beyond our capabilities of
> solving them place us at God's complete mercy."

"I know you think I'm a control freak, but it's never been because I'm power mad," I told her. "It's always and only been because I'm afraid. I want you to be safe, and I don't know how to let go."

She said she didn't know that and she forgave me. Then I told her to have a good time—and I refrained from saying, "Be careful," which was a miracle on par with God parting the Red Sea, if you want to know the truth.

## The Reason It Snowed in Houston on Christmas 2004

I am a control freak. I am a neighbor lady. I hate trusting God. I am afraid to trust God.

The Bible says, "There is no fear in love. But perfect love drives out fear, because fear has to do with punishment. The one who fears is not made perfect in love" (1 John 4:18). My lack of trust stems from fear, which stems from not believing that God truly loves me. I believe that my husband loves me, and as imperfect as he is, I completely trust him to do what's best for me.

So why can't—won't—I trust God, whose love is perfect? Sometimes I feel sorry for God, having to deal with people like me.

Long after Laura had gone to Atlanta safely and back, I still had—I still have—moments of neighbor ladyness, and especially one day in January. It was a Sunday and I had gone to church freaked out with worry and anxiety, trying to control Laura's life with mental telepathy. (I had more or less stopped trying to do it with my cell phone.) She was having car insurance problems or something, and I was in maximum fix-it-myself overdrive. I had been awake worrying most of the night and sat in church listening to my heart pound, which made me even more anxious, so I had to breathe deep and slow to calm myself down. And then I started crying, which I hate doing in church, but what can you do?

*So, why can't—won't—I trust God, whose love is perfect? Sometimes I feel sorry for God, having to deal with people like me.*

Maybe it was something the pastor said, or maybe it was God whispering in my ear, but I remembered that it had snowed in Houston for Christmas. On New Year's Eve, Laura's dearest childhood friend, Kelly, had died of leukemia. At her funeral, the chaplain had said that Kelly had had two last wishes: to have her family together at Christmas and to see snow.

Kelly had been staying in Houston for a last-ditch treatment effort, and her entire family flew there to be with her for Christmas. As for snow, it hadn't snowed on Christmas in Houston for about a hundred years, the chaplain said. But it did a week before Kelly died.

That's why I cried at church. I cried because God cared enough for a dying young woman to make it snow just for her, and I knew, I just knew, that if He would do that, then He would take care of Laura and Alison and Caroline and my sister, Peggy, and everybody else I love, and He would take care of me, too.

That's not saying bad things won't happen, only that God will never leave me nor forsake me; He will never leave me without hope or without peace. His perfect love will drive out my fear. I just need to believe it. The only other option is to be a lunatic.

*His perfect love will drive out my fear. I just need to believe it. The only other option is to be a lunatic.*

The last time Laura was home, we talked about struggle. She was the one who told me that it was necessary, even good. We were at the airport, and as we said good-bye, I tried not to, but I gave it one last shot. "What if I make a list of everything I think you should do with your life and then you can do it and then I'll be happy and leave you alone?" I asked her.

She laughed, and then she said no. And I went home glad that she did.

# Think on These Things

*Think:* What qualities make a person trustworthy? Who in your life has these qualities?

*Study:* What does the Bible say about trust? Look up as many Scriptures as you can (there are many!), and write down the ones that are most meaningful to you in a journal, notebook, or on index cards. Whenever you start to fear and distrust God, read over these Scriptures until your heart is calmed.

Here are some to get you started: Psalm 28:6–9; 55:22; 56:3; Matthew 7:7–11; John 14:27; Romans 15:13.

*Apply:* With a dictionary and thesaurus or other reference helps (check out free online sites), do a word study defining and comparing the following words:

Trust

Worry

Faith

Faithfulness

Next, think of a situation in which you have difficulty trusting God. As they relate to God and His character, how can these words apply to your situation?

*Consider:* How great is God's love for you? Psalm 139 describes God's intimate knowledge and many precious thoughts concerning each of His children.

Matthew 6:25–34 gives us a picture of God's care.

Ephesians 1 speaks about how we are chosen and called and included in Christ.

Romans 8 tells us that God is for us and nothing can separate us from His love.

Read and ponder these three passages. How can these holy Scriptures help you trust God more readily?

*Meditate:* "Did God save you so you would fret? Would he teach you to walk just to watch you fall? Would he be nailed to the cross for your sins and then disregard your prayers? Come on. Is Scripture teasing us when it reads, 'He has put his angels in charge of you to watch over you wherever you go' (Psalm 91:11)? I don't think so either." —Max Lucado, *In the Grip of Grace*

# Chapter Four

# Whirling Dervishly

## When you're frantic and frenzied

*All human evil comes from a single cause,*
*man's inability to sit still in a room.*

BLAISE PASCAL, SEVENTEENTH-CENTURY PHILOSOPHER

When I was a kid I ran away a lot, although I never went far. Besides, my running away was mostly done for dramatic effect. I'd huff out of the house because of some perceived slight, like my youngest brother calling me an albino gorilla or something equally benign and juvenile.

I would usually run to the end of our block and around the corner and sit against the cement wall at Rusty Smith's house until my older brother came to get me or I got bored of being greatly offended. Besides, drama queens need an audience, and there usually wasn't one next to Rusty's wall.

My mom and dad would roll their eyes at me when I came back, although that's not the welcome I would have preferred.

Sometimes I wonder why my parents never sold me to the circus. I'll have to ask them sometime.

I don't remember if I ran away as a teenager, but I did once about ten years ago. It was Mother's Day, and my husband was out mowing the lawn and the girls were either busy or not even home. Like a born-again eleven-year-old drama queen, I stormed out of the house, got in my car, and ran away to McDonald's, although for the life of me I can't remember what set me off.

But there I was at McDonald's, reading a magazine and wondering if my family had already called the FBI to report me missing. After about an hour or so, when I thought my family would be sufficiently penitent, I returned home, fully expecting to find the driveway lined with police cars and concerned neighbors consoling my distraught husband and children. "On Mother's Day, no less," they would say. "Oh, the horror! Oh, the bitter irony!"

> *Like a born-again eleven-year-old drama queen,*
> *I stormed out of the house, got in my car,*
> *and ran away to McDonald's, although for*
> *the life of me I can't remember what set me off.*

But Barry was still mowing the lawn—the turkey—and the girls weren't even home, so no one had even known I was gone, which defeats the purpose of running away. No weeping and wailing and calling a press conference equal a wasted effort. Consequently, I have since stopped running away from my family. Now I just run away from God.

## Still Learning

For the most part, I think that God must have a great time being God. I think He enjoys being a King of irony, a Prince of upside-down-ness.

Take my Bible verse for the year.

Several years ago I started to notice that around November-December-January a Bible verse would begin to emerge in my consciousness and subtly announce itself as my verse for the year, the one that I would roll over in my thoughts and would become my focus throughout the next ten or twelve months. It usually had something to do with my life circumstances, although I often didn't know that until halfway into the year, as if the verse was part of the preparation for what I would be facing.

*For the most part, I think that God must have a great time being God.*

I've never sought out one particular verse; rather, these verses have always seemed to seek me out. I recognize the "it" verse by its everywhereness—on billboards, in books I pick up and leaf through, on greeting cards sent to me by friends, in unexpected and unsought-after places.

My first verse, Ephesians 3:20, came during the year my husband was depressed. Whenever I started feeling despair, this verse would tap me on the shoulder or whisper itself in my ear, "[God] is able to do immeasurably more than all we ask or imagine, according to his power that is at work within us." Sometimes it would shout at me to keep believing that God is so very able.

Another year's verse, "For nothing is impossible with God" (Luke 1:37), became my focus the year my daughter, Laura, left home. I would learn something about her life that would cause me to hyperventilate, and just as I was about to go into lunatic mom overdrive mode, this verse would remind me that this is the same message that the angel told Mary when he announced that she, a virgin, was about to conceive and give birth to the Son of God. If God could do that impossible thing, He could certainly take care of my daughter just fine without my interference.

One year's verse was the passage in John's Gospel where Jesus is talking to a man named Nicodemus about the wind. Jesus tells him that it "blows wherever it pleases" (John 3:8) and likens it to the way the Holy Spirit moves in a person's life. We can feel and see the effects, but we can't direct or control it.

That year my secret Santa at work gave me a set of wind chimes, which I hung in my living room instead of outside, where normal people hang wind chimes. I wanted to know that when and if I ever heard their delicate tinkling, it wouldn't be from just any old wind blowing through the trees, but from the holy wind of God blowing supernaturally through my home, where I needed to experience it most. Ironically, that was also the year four hurricanes blew through Florida.

> *I hung the wind chimes in my living room instead of outside so that when and if I ever heard their delicate tinkling, it wouldn't be from just any old wind blowing through the trees, but from the holy wind of God.*

This brings me to this year's verse, which I don't like, which I don't want, which, frankly, terrifies me: "Be still, and know that I am God" (Psalm 46:10).

The other verses are ones of comfort and warm fuzzies. "God is able." *Yes!* "Immeasurably more." *Amen, brother!* "Nothing's impossible." *Preach it, sister!*

"Be still." *Uh…no thanks.*

If anything, I am the poster child for anti-stillness. I don't like being still; I don't want to be still; being still terrifies me.

For the longest time I tried to resist that verse, as if I could thwart God's plan to teach my heart this very word of holy Scripture by refusing to acknowledge it. I had hoped maybe God would change His mind. Let me have a do-over or let me choose my own verse.

For example, "Let us then approach the throne of grace with confidence, so that we may receive mercy…" (Hebrews 4:16). I like that one—grace, mercy, approaching thrones with confidence. But being still is not a concept I warm up to easily. So, I decided to boycott this verse, hoping that it would leave me alone.

It didn't. It wouldn't. I confided my fear to my friend Penny, and she offered her condolences.

*I am the poster child for anti-stillness. I don't like being still; I don't want to be still; being still terrifies me.*

"I know what you mean," she said. "I'm afraid that if I'm not still on my own, God will make me still—like put me in a body cast so I can't go anywhere."

"That's what I think, too," I told her. I felt ashamed, but what could I do? It was the truth.

That's when I may have heard God sigh, but I wasn't sure. The sigh was in the way you might sigh when, as your toddler is in the middle of a meltdown from being overtired, you try to grab her and hold her and calm her down, but she won't let you. You sigh, not so much because you're angry, but because you want your tornadic storm of a little one to know that your touch is gentle, your words are kind, your thoughts toward her are thoughts of love and not harm. However, because she's whirling out of control, she can't hear you.

You sigh because you know that if she could be still for just a moment, just long enough to hear your voice reassuring her that she's yours and that you'll never leave her nor forsake her no matter how far or fast she runs, if she could just be still for a moment, then maybe she would stop bumping her head on the floor, stop hurting herself.

Like I said, I may have heard God sigh, but probably not, since you need to be still to hear something as soft as a sigh. And because I wasn't still, because I missed God's sigh, I went on a bender instead.

## A Purple Chenille Peace

Actually, before I went on a bender, I had resigned myself to accepting the being still and knowing that God is God verse. That happened after an encounter with a Hindu yogi.

As part of my job at the newspaper, I cover local religion, which means all religions, not just Christianity. Sometimes that means talking to people with worldviews diametrically opposite to mine, such as the young woman who ran a yoga retreat out of her home.

*I may have heard God sigh, but probably not, since you need to be still to hear something as soft as a sigh.*

When I walked into her house and looked around at the pictures on the wall and the various statues and the books on the shelves, I knew I was out of my element. I confess, I had made up my mind beforehand not to like her, but I did like her. I liked her a lot. And even though her Eastern way of thinking and believing collided with my Western Christian beliefs, God used her to speak to me. He can do that, you know.

Walking into her house was walking into stillness. No TV, no radio. No commotion. She spoke so very quietly, slowly, deliberately. Gently, softly. It drove me crazy.

*Come on, honey, pick up the pace*, I wanted to say.

But she continued talking, sitting erect, taking her time. She even breathed, which is often something I forget to do.

After a while I began to slow down, too, and I heard goats outside and a cat's paws treading on her tile floor. It was so quiet that I heard a cat's paws! And even though I could never agree with her core beliefs about the nature of God, she had a stillness about her, and I found myself telling her about my struggle with the "be still" Scripture. She smiled and told me that it was good, that stillness is good and that it would be okay—that I would be okay if I tried it. That it wouldn't kill me.

In that stillness I sensed a voice from heaven's throne saying, "See, I told you so."

But on the way home my restlessness returned, and the more I thought about being still long enough to know that God is God, the more un-still I became. That's what sent me on the bender.

> *In that stillness I sensed a voice from heaven's throne saying, "See, I told you so."*

It wasn't a drinking bender, although I'm beginning to understand what it must be like for an alcoholic to make vows and promises to God to stop drinking and then not be able to do it. Or it's like shopping, like passing your favorite discount store and telling yourself, "Don't go in," but you go in anyway. Telling yourself, "Look, but don't touch," then you touch. "Touch, but don't buy," but you buy anyway.

You buy stuff that you know you don't need and don't really want, but at the moment you're convinced that you can't possibly live without it. Not only that, you can't imagine how you've managed to survive this long without it. So you plunk your money on the counter and drink down whatever it is that you hold in your hand, and you breathe deeply and savor each flicker of brain energy or whatever it is that happens up there inside your head that makes you happy, or at least numb, if only for that instant.

*Ahhhhh.*

But then later you throw up or yell at your kid or do something that you're ashamed of. Outwardly, you blame the booze or you blame your spouse or your boss, or even God, but inwardly, in rare moments when you can't escape your real self, you blame yourself for being such a loser and failing to keep your promise yet again.

I had gone on a bender, a search for serenity and tranquillity. It seems the older I get, the more my insides scream out for peace. I had started with my house, clearing counters of clutter and stripping walls and shelves of stuff. I had decided to fill the empty spaces with simplicity and colors that are soothing on the eye—sand, taupe, eggplant, goldenrod, sage, wheat. Clear glass, plain surfaces, and woven textures. I'd become almost furious in my attempt to fill my house with peace. A whirling dervish for tranquillity.

I had gone shopping for serenity.

> *I'd become almost furious in my attempt to fill my house with peace. A whirling dervish for tranquility.*

In a *Seinfeld* episode, George Costanza's father, Frank, the most un-serene person on the planet, is squished in the backseat of a car, hollering at his wife to slide her seat forward. He yells, "Like an animal—because of her, I have to sit here like an animal! Serenity now! Serenity now!"

Then he explains that a doctor had given him a relaxation tape that instructs him to chant, "Serenity now," whenever his blood pressure gets too high.

George asks, "Are you supposed to yell it?"

"The man on the tape wasn't specific," Frank says.

But God is specific when He says, "Be still, and know that

I am God," although as I raced through the mall I couldn't hear Him. Instead, I felt like Frank Costanza as I shopped for things that I hoped would bring me peace and tranquillity. No one could hear me shouting, "Serenity now!" but shouting I was.

The last item on my list was a purple chenille throw blanket for the chair in my bedroom, as if purple chenille would finally quiet my restlessness.

## Bracelet Epiphanies

The problem with a quest for a purple chenille throw blanket in springtime—aside from the obvious, that not even a dozen blankets would ever quell my restlessness—is that the stores in Florida have long put away their blankets to make room for summer stuff. This only made me more unstill and restless and downright snappy. In times like that I often feel like I could bite somebody, or at least growl or bark. It's not something I'm proud of.

> *The last item on my list was a purple chenille throw blanket for the chair in my bedroom, as if purple chenille would finally quiet my restlessness.*

Seventeenth-century philosopher Blaise Pascal once said that all human evil results from us not being able to sit still in a room. God once said and still says, "Be still." He says, "In repentance and rest is your salvation, in quietness and trust is your strength" (Isaiah 30:15).

But when your mind won't be still, you forget that. You think that your strength and your soul-satisfaction and your meaning and contentment are found in activity and the pursuit of that next thing on your list.

Just recently, my biggest pursuit in life was bracelets. It's what

I thought about when I woke up in the morning and what I thought about as my head hit the pillow at night. I would be ashamed if I were to tally up the hundreds of dollars and equally as many hours that I spent buying and stringing beads. Eventually, I wore myself out doing it. I had filled a glass jar on my bathroom counter with bracelets of every bead color combination imaginable, "my pretties" I called them. Finally, when I could no longer stuff another bracelet in my jar, in a rare moment of sanity and clarity I actually said out loud, "This does not satisfy my soul!"

To which I sensed a voice from heaven answer, "Duh."

That was all it took for me to run to my big recliner chair next to my back living room window, which is my God chair. It's where, when I allow myself, I am still. It's where the tornadic toddler goes when she finally stops her frenzy long enough to let her Father's gentle touch and whispered words calm the whirlwind that's inside.

It's where I let God remind me that my life isn't found in the plastic boxes of beads under my bed, but in Him. And at that moment I tasted life in His stillness, and I knew I was foolish to try to find life anywhere else.

*When I could no longer stuff another bracelet in my jar, in a rare moment of sanity and clarity I actually said out loud, "This does not satisfy my soul!"*

But the day that I went searching for the purple chenille blanket I had forgotten about my bracelet epiphany; I tend to do that. I tend to forget what I know is true, that the Lord is my shepherd and I shall not want because He leads me beside still waters and restores my soul (Psalm 23). I forget that He stills the roaring of the seas, the roaring of the waves, and the turmoil of the nations

(Psalm 65:7). I forget that He quiets me, not with a Taser gun or bug zapper, but with His love (Zephaniah 3:17).

It's when I forget all that, when I forget that God is for me, not against me, that I go off on purple chenille benders.

## Mercy Carved in Stone

When I'm honest, I have to admit that one of the things I like best about God is His relentless pursuit of His runaway children. Even as I run from Him, I'm always pleading for Him to come and find me. I think that would be the worst possible thing that could ever happen, to run away and have no one come after you.

Even so, it's hard to shake the image of God that I had as a child: stern and angry, like the big-head-no-body "great and terrible" Wizard of Oz. And if God/Oz said to "be still," it could only mean you were about to be fried. That's why I fought so hard to not have the "be still" verse be mine for the year—I was afraid, and fear makes me run.

*Even as I run from Him, I'm always pleading for Him to come and find me.*

There's an episode of *Little House on the Prairie* that is forever etched on my soul. It's the one where Albert, the adopted son of Ma and Pa Ingalls, sneaks a smoke in the basement of the blind school where his sister Mary teaches. The pipe starts a fire, the school burns down, and Mary's baby dies in the fire. Wracked with guilt, fear, and shame, Albert takes off running—with Pa in hot, relentless pursuit after him, calling his name, shouting for him to stop running.

Albert runs, certain that if he stopped long enough, Pa would catch up with him and that would be the end. Pa would probably kill him, or worse. Pa might tell Albert he was no longer his son. Un-adopt him.

So Albert runs and runs and runs, and at the climax of Albert's terror and exhaustion, just as Pa is close enough to overtake him, the father calls out to this child who has caused so much heartache and destruction, "Son! I love you!"

It's the second most incredible snapshot of mercy that I've ever seen, the first being the crucifixion of Jesus. To have the Son of God die the very death I deserve and then not require anything from me except faith—I still don't know why I would think that God wants to harm me. I still don't know why, when He says "stop" that I think it's because He wants to hurt me. Just like I don't know why my parents never sold me to the circus, I also don't know why God doesn't just let me keep running until I hit a wall and knock myself unconscious. Then *He* could sell me to the circus.

But He doesn't. In His mercy, He runs after me, which sometimes makes me think, "Is He nuts?"

*To have the Son of God die the very death I deserve and then not require anything from me except faith—I still don't know why I would think that God wants to harm me.*

Back to my desperate pursuit of a purple chenille blanket. I eventually found one, but not before mercy found me and stopped me from running. On a clearance table, way in the back of a discount store, was a stone cross with the word MERCY engraved in it.

Mercy carved in stone for $2.49.

It was simple, rugged and rustic, and fit my décor. I don't know how long I stood there, clinging to that cross of mercy, just staring at it, drinking in its message, but as I did I thought about a chorus that I had learned as a new Christian: "Be still and know that I am God; come unto Me for My burden is easy and light."

That second part is taken from an invitation that Jesus extends to weary and burdened folks to come to Him and learn from Him, to cast their cares upon Him, for He is "gentle and humble in heart" and offers rest (Matthew 11:28–30).

Although I'm never sure of the protocol for worshiping in a discount store, I couldn't help it. What else can you do when you're clinging to a cross of mercy and God shows up, bringing stillness and rest with Him? I started singing, and as I sang I considered that maybe being still and knowing that God is God isn't so terrible and that maybe God's not out to flatten me but to give me peace in my unpeaceful soul and quietness in my restless heart.

*Although I'm never sure of the protocol for worshiping in a discount store, I couldn't help it.*

I also considered that maybe my Scripture verse for the year was a two-in-one, psalm and gospel, command and invitation, and that maybe stillness really was good. Maybe I really would be okay.

Just for a moment, there in the back of that discount store, my soul quieted. It was just for a moment, but it was good.

# Think on These Things

*Think:* Think of a time when you've been frenzied and frantic. Next, think of a time when you've been still (or imagine such a time). Contrast each scenario by describing the sights and sounds and smells. Describe your thoughts and your feelings. What are the physical, emotional, and spiritual benefits of being still?

*Study:* Using a Bible concordance, look up the Scriptures that use words like *rest, quiet, quietness, still, stilled, stillness*. What is going on in each passage? Who is using the words, and to whom are they directed?

Choose one or two passages that particularly speak to you, and look them up in several different Bible translations and paraphrases for nuances of meaning.

*Apply:* Whenever you feel yourself becoming restless, unstill, and disquieted, go back to those Scriptures and consider how to apply them to your life. What is an attribute or characteristic of God that can help you slow down and rest in Him?

If memorizing and learning Scripture seems too overwhelming, ask God to give you one verse to focus on for the year (or month or week).

*Consider:* In Psalm 65:7, the writer says that God "stilled the roaring of the seas, the roaring of their waves, and the turmoil of the nations." Likewise, in Psalm 107:29, the writer says that God "stilled the storm to a whisper; the waves of the sea were hushed."

But in Psalm 131:2, the writer says, "But I have stilled and quieted my soul; like a weaned child with its mother."

In some cases, God does the quieting, yet in this case, the writer quiets himself. What are some ways that you can quiet yourself, even in the midst of turmoil?

*Meditate:* "I am serene because I know thou lovest me. Because thou lovest me, naught can move me from my peace. Because thou lovest me, I am as one to whom all good has come." —Alistair Maclean, *God in Our Midst*

# Chapter Five

# The Exquisite Pain of Desire
## When you long for more

*And I still haven't found what I'm looking for.*

U 2

At some point it hits you. This is it.

*This is my life, and it's a real possibility that things will never be any different.*

*This is my marriage—good, not great. Moments of satisfaction, months of disappointment.*

Or: *It's difficult and I want out, or at least a change. It's not how it was in the beginning, and I want it back. It's tense, blah, lifeless, loveless.*

Or: *I'm single. There is no one with whom I will ever share my life. I will never know sex unless it's illicit. I will live alone with my cats and my plants and tell myself that everything is okay, when deep inside it's not. I long to be married and I'm not.*

*I'm. Just. Not.*

Or: *Ever since I can remember I've wanted to be a mother, to watch my belly grow, to feel that first kick. Yet, despite my longing to bear a child, to raise and nurture a family, I will never have this longing fulfilled.*

*At some point it hits you. This is it.*

Fill in the blanks with what haunts you—memories of your childhood that will never bring a smile. Regrets that you wish would go away. Children who aren't who you had hoped they would be. Even a life that is, for the most part, good.

And yet.

That's the problem in a nutshell. It's the "and yet" that is so troubling.

*My life is good*, you think, *and yet, despite my contentment, despite my gratitude, despite my thankfulness for all that's good and challenging, perplexing and even difficult, despite knowing that my life has purpose and meaning, despite all that, deep within there's an ache for something more. Something else, something beyond, something other—a vague sense of yearning, a soul-stretching, as if my soul had arms that flailed, reaching frantically for…what?*

*It's as if…if I could just touch whatever it is that I'm longing and yearning for, if I could glimpse it, grasp it. Maybe if I could put a name to it, maybe it would lessen, maybe even go away so I could stop feeling so guilty for wanting it.*

In a *Seinfeld* episode, Kramer asks George, "Do you ever yearn?"

George: "Yearn? Do I yearn?"

Kramer: "I yearn."

George: "You yearn."

Kramer: "Oh, yes. Yes, I yearn. Often, I…I sit…and yearn. Have you yearned?"

George: "Well, not recently. I craved. I crave all the time, constant craving. But I haven't yearned."

## Welcome to My (MTM) World

I can't think of a time that I haven't yearned. When I was younger, I yearned to be someone else—anyone else. I wanted to have blue eyes and blond hair and long legs. I wanted to be a dancer and a stewardess and drink martinis with men in tuxedos.

I wanted to live on a Greek island and fall in love with a Greek man who didn't speak English but who loved me and thought I was beautiful.

*I can't think of a time that I haven't yearned.*

At one time I wanted to be Mary Tyler Moore. Not so much MTM the actress, but Mary Richards, the character she played on her television show. I used to lie on my bed and imagine myself working in a newsroom, living in my own apartment, having meaningful relationships with quirky but loyal co-workers and friends.

I wanted to be someone's quirky and loyal friend.

Since I wasn't too crazy about the idea of living in Minnesota like Mary Richards did, I tweaked my MTM fantasy a bit and moved it to New York City and daydreamed about shopping at neighborhood markets, asking Joe the Produce Guy if he recommended the cherries from Washington state this year or if I should stick with buying bananas.

In my daydreams, I dined out with friends after an evening performance of the most current Broadway show, as I imagined MTM would do. I even bought myself a ceramic *N* like the *M* that Mary Richards had hanging on her wall.

At one point I think I spent more of my waking hours living my MTM existence inside my thoughts than I did living my real life. Whenever I would start fixating on the meaninglessness and hopelessness of not just my life, but life in general, I'd *poof!* myself into MTM World.

I used to wonder if that's how mental illness started. I used to wonder if maybe I was not normal—and what exactly is normal anyway? Is it normal to want something else? Is it normal to feel that this is not enough, that you were created for another world, another reality, another existence?

Those were my questions at the time, and I didn't like asking them. I didn't like the wanting and the longing for something that I couldn't grasp. What I wanted didn't even have a name or a label. I couldn't describe it, couldn't wrap my brain around it. It was too big, too nebulous, too other.

*Is it normal to feel that this is not enough,*
*that you were created for another world,*
*another reality, another existence?*

I could only lie on my bed and long for it or stare out the window and search the skies for it.

But if I had to put a name to it, what I really wanted back then was to feel the feeling MTM felt when she tossed her hat into the air during the opening credits as the theme song assured her that she was "gonna make it after all."

*That's* what I wanted! A theme song and a promise that I, too, would make it after all. That I would find a reason to get up in the morning and a reason to toss my hat in the air.

And so I yearned.

Do you yearn?

Recently, I asked some friends to write down their yearnings.

Here's what some of them wrote:

- I yearn to trust God enough that when a crisis is looming, I won't have my heart jumping out of my chest. After a crisis, I always tell myself that the *next* time, I will give it all to the Lord, but the *next* time comes and there I go again, getting all upset. I would have hoped that by the time I reached this beautiful age of seventy, I'd have it all put together. (Yeah, right!)
- I yearn to see our daughter, son-in-law, and granddaughters really know the love of their Father and not just go through the motions of simply going to church. I also yearn to live long enough to know that a beautiful friend in Christ will be reconciled with her son. She has all but given up hope.
- I yearn, from the deepest places of my soul, for my youngest son to become a Christian. I've tried bargaining about this with God (like He bargains), going so far as to ask Him to take my life if that's what it would take for my son to turn to Jesus.
- Our family is so dysfunctional, and I yearn for a normal, close family relationship. You know, like *Leave It to Beaver*.
- I yearn for sweet intimacy with my husband—a closeness that includes more than talking about problems or regrets. I want to share dreams, to trust, to think of him with loving desire, for us to be each other's best friend instead of the arguing and hurting, the withdrawal and complacency from him.
- No matter how hard I try, I don't think I will ever have the close, intimate, personal, and long-lasting relationship with my daughter-in-law that I want. Since I don't have a daughter, which is what I really yearn for, I thought I could find it with her, but I don't think it's possible.
- I'm average, and I yearn to be excellent.

The problem is, at least as I see it, you start out wanting one thing—to be Mary Tyler Moore or to be rich or to meet the Yankees' first baseman or to find a soul mate over the Internet. You start out with your list: you want curly hair and straight teeth, less stress and more time, to be wildly cherished and madly adored, to be excellent, to be normal, to be functional.

You start out thinking that you know what you want, what you really, really want, and that if you could only have this one thing, or maybe just three out of the top ten things on your want list, you're sure that you could be—that you would be—content.

You start out asking God: "Please, just give me (insert your request here), and I promise I won't want anything else." But then you want and you want and you want, and you keep on wanting until you think your wanting, like thirsting in the desert, will surely drive you mad if it doesn't kill you first.

And the wanting makes you feel guilty because after all that Jesus has done for you, that should surely be enough. So you tell yourself to just suck it up and be a man or whatever and quit whining.

Quit wanting. Quit longing and pining and yearning for that thing that has no name, or the thing that has a name but is out of your reach.

*The wanting makes you feel guilty because after all that Jesus has done for you, that should surely be enough. So you tell yourself to just suck it up and be a man or whatever and quit whining.*

But you can't unwant something you want. You can't unyearn.

## When Wanting More Is Good

I haven't quite figured this out yet, so please bear with me, but I think there's something that's quite good about yearning. I'm not talking about lusting and coveting and wanting a Lexus when you can barely afford a Ford Focus, or about daydreaming about Greek men when you're married to an Irish-Italian from New York.

I'm talking about that almost exquisite pain of desire, that sweetness to the stabbing agony of wanting and longing for what you've never experienced, yet what you sense you've somehow been created for. It's such a sweet pain that it makes you groan.

It's that anticipation of an ideal, the imagining of something perfectly satisfying. It's the wanting of wanting no more. It's the certainty of the moment when the waiter asks, "Would you like anything else?" and of being able to answer, "No, thank you. I'm full," without having second thoughts about the Mississippi mud pie and if only you hadn't ordered the baked potato you would have room in your belly for just a sliver.

The Bible talks about all of creation groaning. Elm trees and parsnips and angelfish and ragweed, people and penguins and the Indian Ocean, all groan in anticipation of something greater, grander, more, other.

"The created world itself can hardly wait for what's coming next," writes the apostle Paul to the people in the church in Rome. "Everything in creation is being more or less held back. God reins it in until both creation and all the creatures are ready and can be released at the same moment into the glorious times ahead. Meanwhile, the joyful anticipation deepens" (Romans 8:19–21, *The Message*).

It's as if the more we groan, the deeper our longing, and the more intense our yearning, the more alive we become.

In *Till We Have Faces*, C. S. Lewis writes, "It was when I was happiest that I longed most…. The sweetest thing in all my life has been the longing…to find the place where all the beauty came from."

When I have deep questions that might or might not have answers, I always ask my uncle-dad. Sometimes he knows answers; mostly he just lets me ask my questions until I figure stuff out for myself.

> *It's as if the more we groan, the deeper our longing, and the more intense our yearning, the more alive we become.*

I asked him once about this yearning for the thing that doesn't have a name, whether it's a sin to want more, to not be satisfied and to carry around a gnawing discontent. Like I said, you can't unwant what you want, and you can't unyearn a yearning.

He told me that right now his life is good, but that sometimes before bed he thinks, *Is there something better?* And then he wonders where that comes from—is it from God or is it from somewhere else, somewhere darker?

He said that he thinks it's from God. "That's how you know that He exists," he said.

In the Bible, King Solomon wrote that God "has planted eternity in men's hearts and minds [a divinely implanted sense of a purpose working through the ages which nothing under the sun but God alone can satisfy]" (Ecclesiastes 3:11, AMP).

So God Himself has planted in us the yearning, the groaning for something more, something better than this.

"It's a gift from Him and it's good, because it points us to Him and to a time when everything will be fixed," my uncle-dad told me.

That's all well and good and future and all, but what about

now? What about here on earth? What about the groanings that you and I have that don't seem to go away?

## But Not Quite

My husband and I have been married for more than thirty years, and I still haven't figured out why we've lasted that long. I suppose the short answer is "because of God," and I imagine that if I think about it too much, that will still be the only answer I can come up with.

Barry and I had only known each other for four months before we got married, and we are widely different in every way imaginable, yet we've found a contentment with each other and a deep enjoyment of each other despite our differences, which have included being mismatched in matters of Christian faith for most of our married life.

It has always been a longing, a yearning, to share with my husband the experience of worship and of being loved by Jesus, and there have been times.

But not quite.

> *What about the groanings that you and*
> *I have that don't seem to go away?*

I remember meeting a woman who lamented that her "spiritually unequal" marriage, as she called it, made her feel hopelessly unfulfilled. Then she began telling me that, although her husband was a Christian, although he led their family in matters of faith, although he was a leader in the church, a good provider, kind and full of grace, although they sang together in a Christian band and prayed together, she thought there should be more.

I wanted to deck her. I know women who live with husbands

who hate their Christian faith, who make life hell on earth for their wives, and this woman was moaning because her marriage was not quite.

"Are you nuts?" I wanted to say.

And yet, her yearning was real.

Just like "and yet," there's a "not-quite-ness" to our souls. Even if we attain that which we long for, it's never quite it. There's never a finality, a once-and-for-all, an ultimate Snickers moment when every cell, every molecule, every mitochondria of our existence is completely satisfied.

Philosopher Blaise Pascal said, "We are never living, but hoping to live; and whilst we are always preparing to be happy, it is certain, we never shall be so, if we aspire to no other happiness than what can be enjoyed in this life."

I think we instinctively know this to be true, but what do you do with the forty or fifty or eighty or ninety years that you have here on earth? What do you do while you're waiting for heaven? What do you do with the yearnings within you that you can't quiet?

*Just like "and yet," there's a "not-quite-ness" to our souls.*

Jesus Himself said that He came so His followers "may have and enjoy life, and have it in abundance (to the full, till it overflows)" (John 10:10, AMP). He said it, so shouldn't that be true of our experience? That we are full "till it overflows"—no room for Mississippi mud pie? *I couldn't eat another bite, thank you very much.*

Is there a true—maybe *true* isn't the right word—is there a lasting contentment, a place where, if we can just reach it, then the wanting will go away? I think that it's possible to have a true contentment, such as I've found in my marriage, but sometimes I wonder if it will last. (Sometimes I think that I think too much.)

Frankly, I'm almost sorry that I've even brought this subject up, except that I've met too many people who, like me, lie on their beds or stare out their windows and hold their yearnings in their hands, hating them and yet wanting beyond want to satisfy, to appease them, and going nearly insane with guilt for even having them in the first place.

And yet.

And yet I keep coming back to the very sweetness of longing itself, because if it's truly from God, then it's there as a gift, and a gift is always good—if it's from God, anyway.

"Hoping for something is sometimes better than having it," my uncle-dad said once.

At the time I chalked it up to him being of advanced years, but the more I think about it, the more I think he's right, as was C. S. Lewis about longing most in his happiness, wanting to "find the place where all the beauty came from."

## Longing for Home

Sometimes I just want to go home. It's not a death wish or anything like that, or thoughts of suicide. I just want to go home.

And this longing for home is rarely in those moments when life stinks on toast, but almost always when life can't seem to get any better. I'll walk outside in the morning to go to a job I love and be with people I love, and I'll look at the sky, all purple and pink and apricot, and I'll be struck by a sense of God's presence.

*I keep coming back to the very sweetness of longing itself, because if it's truly from God, then it's there as a gift, and a gift is always good—if it's from God, anyway.*

"My Father made that," I'll say to the morning sky, and I'll immediately get an attack of ironic homesickness, of loving life but wanting to go and be with the One whom I've never seen yet whom I love intensely.

My uncle-dad says that if you have your mind on heaven, wanting to one day go home, then you'll do great things on earth. Our longing, like a fly that keeps biting a horse's rump, is the thing that makes us go, he says.

I think he's right. If I had no longing for something more, for that something that we were created for and for that which was imprisoned back when Adam and Eve sinned in the Garden of Eden, if I had an absolute contentment here and now, then why would I write? Why would I read? Why would any of us sing or dance or paint or pray or…?

If our longing for more is the thing that makes us go, if it's the thing that makes us go to Him, again and again and again, then it's a good thing. It's a best thing to have it go unfulfilled.

One day our longings will be fulfilled. One day we will understand.

One day, we who are His will go home. We will see the One for whom our souls yearn.

> *My longing for home is rarely in those moments when life stinks on toast, but almost always when life can't seem to get any better.*

However, until then, there will always be unanswered questions, or muddied and ambivalent answers, maybe even muddied questions. There will always be a not-quite-ness to our souls.

Knowing that makes the yearning bearable. As long as there's a future and a promise and a hope, then it's okay. I might not like it, but as long as there's a one day on the horizon, I'm okay with it.

The Bible talks about the one day when we see Jesus in all His glory and majesty. We will have been given crowns for our good works here on earth, which we will at that time cast at His feet. And we will sing!

> *Because anything that God begins He will certainly complete, I have the promise, unseen yet sure.*

Maybe my MTM fantasy wasn't so far off base. I had wanted a theme song. I had wanted to toss my hat. I had wanted, and still want, that feeling of having arrived, of attaining, of achieving, of there being no more crying, no more disappointment or emptiness, no more wanting more.

And because anything that God begins He will certainly complete, I have the promise, unseen yet sure.

I'm "gonna make it after all."

# Think on These Things

*Think:* When you lie on your bed or stare out a window, where do your thoughts go? What is it that you want and yearn for?

*Study:* Read the story of Jacob and his wives, Rachel and Leah, in Genesis 29–30:24. Imagine that you are Leah, and describe your longing. If you were Rachel, what would you long for? How did God comfort each of them?

*Apply:* Read Hebrews 11. Take note of verses 13–16 and 39–40. When you think of your own longings, how can these verses comfort you? See also the following verses in 2 Corinthians—1:18–22; 4:16–18; 9:8; and 12:8–10.

*Consider:* From *The Valley of Vision*, part of a Puritan prayer says, "Blessed Lord, let me climb up near to thee, and love, and long, and plead, and wrestle with thee, and pant for deliverance from the body of sin, for my heart is wandering and lifeless, and my soul mourns to think it ever should lose sight of its beloved."

It is a good thing to wrestle with God, not as a foe, but as a child seeking comfort from a loving Father.

*Meditate:* "To sustain the life of the heart, the life of deep desire, we desperately need to possess a clearer picture of the life that lies before us." —John Eldredge, *The Journey of Desire*

# Chapter Six

# Praying Through the Seaweed

### When your life goes awry

*Behind every headline is a purpose of God,*
*even if it's hidden from us.*

ERWIN LUTZER, *RUNNING TO WIN* RADIO PROGRAM

I call it the year the darkness swallowed us whole. You would have to know my husband to fully appreciate the irony of what happened.

Barry is a no-stress, easygoing, *que sera sera* kind of guy. He's fun and low-maintenance, steady, and rock-solid. You can count on him.

That's why when the darkness came and chose him as its target, as if depression had a will of its own, it took all of us who know him by surprise. We never dreamed it could or would happen to him, and we didn't see it coming until it had fully engulfed us all.

Although it was his depression, because I'm his wife, it was mine as well. At the time he was working out of town and had been coming home on weekends, but as the darkness fell and choked and tormented, he began staying away for longer stretches of time, weeks and weeks and weeks.

When he did come home, he stayed to himself. He had climbed inside himself and disappeared, and the Barry that was left on the outside, with its angry eyes and bitter words, was not the Barry we had always known. This Barry talked of death, of leaving, of remorse and regret, of wanting those who love him to not be burdened with him any longer.

*Although it was his depression, because I'm his wife, it was mine as well.*

For the first time in our married life, he did not want me, and sometimes at night I would slip away to the dock at the lake nearby our house and search for stars, as if they held answers to my confusion and my fear.

I would sit and listen to the black water lapping the shore and stare into the even blacker sky and beg God to come and lift the darkness—but it remained.

A breeze would blow against my cheeks wet from tears, and I would simultaneously curse God for His cruelty and reach out for His hand. I would tell myself, "We will get through this; we will get to the other side," all the while doubting that there would even be an other side.

Barry himself would tell me that I was crazy to stay with him, that he might always be this way and the best thing for me to do was leave and try to find happiness elsewhere.

Weeks turned into months and the darkness remained, continuing to choke the life out of us, like we were adrift in a vast, deep ocean, with seaweed wrapped around our heads and a current pulling us under.

*A breeze would blow against my cheeks wet from tears, and I would simultaneously curse God for His cruelty and reach out for His hand.*

I'm on staff at a newspaper here in Florida and write a weekly column, Grace Notes. As the darkest of the darkness descended, it was December and I had a Christmas column to write. So I penned these words:

It's Christmas…and life has kicked you in the gut. It gave you a sucker punch and knocked the breath right out of you. Maybe you saw it coming and braced yourself for the impact. Maybe it blindsided you. Either way, you're left crumpled in a heap on the floor.

And it's Christmas.

A call at midnight announces bad news.

The doctor tells you, "The test results don't look good."

Your stocks take a nosedive. You lose your job. Your child's in jail.

Your spouse sits you down and says, "We need to talk," and the news causes your foundation to crumble.

Or maybe you've reached a point in your life where you realize you've squandered everything you've been given. You've messed up. You've hurt the ones you love the most, and you can't go back and undo your mistakes.

And it haunts you.

Especially at Christmas.

So you're crumpled in a heap on the floor, gasping for breath. Wondering, crying, pleading to know: Does God see me? Does He care? Will He come to me, be with me?

But He doesn't come, or so it seems. Your pain gets worse. You're certain the weight of your burdens will surely crush you.

And even though it's Christmas and you're supposed to be filled with peace and joy, you're not. Instead, you're flailing and writing, seeking relief anywhere, everywhere, any way you know how.

*Does God see me? Does He care? Will He come to me, be with me?*

And the universe remains still. Relief doesn't come, only darkness. So you curse the darkness—and you wait. And hope. And hold on.

Because it's Christmas, you mouth the words of a song, the only Christmas song you know that fits your mood: "O come, O come, Emmanuel, and ransom captive Israel."

You don't fully understand its meaning, only that you feel as if you're a captive, too.

Because you are.

## A Seaweed-Wrapped Prophet

His name was Jonah, and he, too, had seaweed wrapped around his head. God had told him to go to the city of Nineveh to preach against the people's wickedness, but Jonah went the other direction and hopped on a boat.

*Then God sent a violent storm.*

Jonah had been sleeping below deck, and the ship's terrified crew woke him up. They had cast lots to see whose god had been ticked off, and the lot fell to Jonah.

Jonah told them that he was a prophet of the almighty God, the One who made and sustains the wind and the waves and who sends violent storms and earthquakes and hurricanes and tsunamis. Jonah added that he was the reason for the storm and that if they threw him overboard all would be calm—at least for them. It meant sure death for him.

Although reluctant at first, the sailors tossed Jonah into the raging sea, and it became calm, which terrified them even more, and they worshiped the God who made the ocean itself.

Then God sent a big fish to swallow Jonah, "and Jonah was inside the fish three days and three nights" (Jonah 1:1–17, my paraphrase).

While inside the fish, with seaweed wrapped around his head, surrounded by darkness and no escape hatch in sight, Jonah prayed. He acknowledged that God was the One who had hurled him into the sea, that He had sent the storm, and that He had sent the fish to swallow him—and at that point, Jonah had no promise of a happy ending. He had been swallowed up into the darkness, and it was at God's hand.

> He acknowledged that God was the One who had hurled him into the sea.

God did it. He sent the storm. He sent the calamity. He sent the fish.

He sends darkness and confusion and terror—and we generally don't like that in our God.

## The Devil's Fingerprints

She had dark hair and dark eyes, and I had offended her deeply, which was not a good way to end an otherwise idyllic weekend. I had been with a group of women, teaching from the Old Testament book of Jonah. It was the last of four sessions at a near-perfect retreat in the North Carolina mountains. It had even snowed a bit.

I had managed to not offend anyone up until then (that I know of). I read the Scripture passage about the storm and the fish and said that they were God's doing from start to finish. Next, I told the women that I liken Jonah's inside-the-fish situation to the unpleasant and downright painful situations in our lives that we hate with all our might. So far so good, no one had picked up a rock to stone me—yet.

> *She had dark hair and dark eyes, and I had offended her deeply, which was not a good way to end an otherwise idyllic weekend.*

Then I said, "These situations—financial difficulties, wayward children, disappointing marriages, chronic pain, maybe even cancer—might be the very things God sends to swallow us in order for Him to work a greater purpose."

The dark-haired woman had cancer.

Although I didn't know it until the session ended, she had run out of the room deeply and furiously offended to think that anyone would say that God has anything to do with evil, sickness, calamity, or disease.

This is something theologians call "theodicy." If God is all-good, all-knowing, and all-powerful, then why does evil or tragedy happen? Does He cause it, or does He merely allow it?

Is God sovereign or is He not?

After the session ended and I learned what had happened, I ran to speak with the woman and to apologize for offending her.

She adamantly opposed what I had said. God doesn't send bad things into people's lives, she insisted. He has nothing to do with them. They're not His intention. Adversity is not His perfect will for His people, and He doesn't cause it. He does, however, allow it, she said.

But is that true? Not "true because that's what we want to be true," but truly true?

King David said of God, "In faithfulness you have afflicted me" (Psalm 119:75). Other Scripture passages imply or state clearly that God sends difficulty and pain, even to His chosen people.

It's not something I like to think about, and it's not an easy question to ask: Does God ordain evil?

Many people say, and I've probably said it myself, "My God wouldn't _____." But is that making "my God" a God other than the biblical God? It's absurd to think we can build a God to our own liking, with interchangeable parts, like a Mr. Potato Head God, and I would think that the real God gets quite ticked at those who would reduce Him to a manageable deity.

Frankly, I don't want a manageable deity. Well, I do, but not really. When my life goes awry, I want to know that Someone bigger and wiser and more powerful than me is in charge. I learned this, theoretically anyway, years ago when my husband was unemployed and I discovered I was pregnant with our daughter Laura.

*It's not something I like to think about and it's not an easy question to ask: Does God ordain evil?*

At the time I remember thinking that either there is no God and everything is utterly out of control, or there is a God who knows exactly what He's doing. I knew that those were my only two options and that they weren't even options. God simply is, and He does exactly, precisely, purposefully, carefully as He has always planned from before eternity.

He has no Plan B, only Plan A. No mistakes, no misses, no errors, no fouls. He never slaps His forehead and says, "How could that have happened?" He never says, "Oops."

I still don't know how He did it, but even with my husband out of work for nearly a year, all of our bills were paid, and we had a place to sleep, food to eat, and lots of extras just because God delights in caring for His kids.

> *I remember thinking that either there is no*
> *God and everything is utterly out of control,*
> *or there is a God who knows exactly what He's doing.*

He proved Himself sovereign as well as good then and since, but even so, when I came home from the retreat after offending the dark-haired woman, I went to talk to my pastor, just in case I had God all wrong. After all, unemployment and seemingly ill-timed pregnancies don't compare with cancer and death and destruction. This was shortly after 9/11. It was the question on a lot of people's minds: If God is good, why does evil happen?

"*Allows* and *sends* are the same thing," my pastor said. "One uses the word *allow* to make the reality of God's sovereignty easier for tender ears. But no circumstance comes that doesn't first pass through His sovereign hands.

"Unless you agree that God ordains everything that happens, either by giving permission or actively causing it, the alternative is that God is powerless to stop something from happening, and if that's true, then we're really in deep weeds," he said. "But even when we admit that fact, we still have to wrestle with this: God allows some really bad things to happen that He can easily prevent."

He said that whenever people come to him with their questions about the goodness of God in the face of evil, he asks them to name the most evil act in history. While most say the Holocaust, he tells them that the single most evil act was the crucifixion of Jesus.

> ☞ *"We might not understand God, but we know that He is good and that He uses sin sinlessly."* ☜

"Why? Because the only person who ever lived a perfect, sinless life, the only person who was ever completely innocent, suffered a horrible, painful death at the hands of evil men—the world's worst murder became the world's only salvation," he said.

He added, "The evil things that men do and the evil that's in the world have the devil's fingerprints all over them, but what Satan purposes for evil and evil alone, God purposes for good. We might not understand God, but we know that He is good and that He uses sin sinlessly."

## Darkness Turns to Dawn

When my friend Angel went through a dark time in her life, she would go out walking early in the morning, well before daylight. She said nothing in her life made sense, and she would pound out her soul on the pavement, crying and praying—mostly crying—and calling out to God.

She did this every morning, and as she wound her way through her neighborhood and through the range of her emotions and jumbled thoughts, the sky would begin to turn from black to purple and pink and orange—and she would gasp.

"Every day the sun rose, each day more spectacular than the one before," she said. "Every day it was like God saying, 'Watch this one—I've got a good one for you today!' And then I'd go home to my messy life, to the pain and the chaos, but I'd keep with me the thought that there is a God, and He hadn't forgotten me."

Likewise, as my friend Mike's life imploded and his twenty-year marriage ended, leaving him separated by 150 miles from the daughter he loves more than life itself, he would often stand on his front porch facing the lake and scream at God.

Mike said that one night he was particularly angry at how his life was going. He had hoped that his divorce would solve his problems, that he could be a clean slate and live alone in his old Florida cracker-style house and write books by the sounds of crickets chirping and frogs croaking, that it would be romantic and idyllic.

*Thunder shook the house, and as lightning struck repeatedly, lighting up the darkened summer sky, he was silenced.*

He hadn't planned on his ex-wife moving away. He hadn't planned on the divorced-parent kid exchange every other weekend and the guilt he felt for his part in the dissolution of his family.

That night, as Mike stood and hurled accusations at God into the black sky, it suddenly began to rain torrents, which is common in Florida.

"Is that the best You've got?" he taunted God.

Next, thunder shook the house, and Mike said that as lightning began to strike repeatedly, lighting up the darkened summer sky, he was silenced. He didn't feel God's anger toward his anger, but a sense that God was saying, "Mike, look what I can do. Is there anything too difficult for Me?"

Mike said he was quieted by God's display of power, and although he hated his present situation, he knew that he would be safe in God's sovereign hands.

## God Comes to Thee

God sees through our darkness. He sees past it, over it, around it, underneath it. He sees its purpose, even if we never do, even if our present darkness lasts a lifetime.

Although the darkness that had swallowed my husband and my family hadn't yet gone when I wrote my Christmas column, this is how I ended it:

It's Christmas, and just when you think there is no hope and you can't hold on any longer.…

God comes to you.

It's Christmas! And He comes and pierces through your darkness and lifts you from the floor. He binds your wounds and eases your pain. He lets you know that He's loved you from eternity. He rejoices over you with singing and pours Himself over you until you are washed from the inside out. He spreads His glory around you and lifts your spirit to a place higher than it has ever known.

It's Christmas—God comes to you.

He kisses you with grace. Calls you by name. He gives you His promise that He will never leave you and seals His covenant with the blood of His own Son.

That little Baby, not in a manger, but pierced and bloodied, hanging on a tree. It's Christmas and God comes to you. Not only that, He continues to come to you again and again and again—but not as a baby. He comes as a warrior, like Mel Gibson in the movie *The Patriot*, with eyes burning with anger. But don't be afraid, because the anger's not toward you. Instead, His white-hot anger is for the darkness that tried to consume you and for the pain that left you crumpled in a heap on the floor.

He comes to you and battles your demons and slays your enemies. And because He's God, He wins. And because He wins, you win, too—because you're His, because He comes to save His own.

It's Christmas! Emmanuel, "God with us," has come.

So you sing the rest of the song: "Rejoice! Rejoice! Emmanuel shall come to thee, O Israel!"

Emmanuel has come to thee. He comes to you.

And when He comes…

Because He's come…

As His glory floods your soul, you know that you know that you know that the Maker of the oceans and the stars has entered your world and has changed you.

And nothing will ever be the same again.


I wrote that in the midst of the darkness, and I would read it over and over, knowing that it was true, even if I didn't see it, and I kept waiting and hoping for the dawn.

It came suddenly one day, although the dawn never really is sudden. Before it appears, it's always just beyond, out of reach and out of sight, but on its way nonetheless, and always on time.

*I wrote that in the midst of the darkness, and I read it over and over, knowing that it was true, even if I didn't see it, and I kept waiting and hoping for the dawn.*

Barry had come home for a visit, which turned out badly. As he left to return to his job, the last thing he said to me was, "Maybe it's best if you divorce me."

Then he was gone, and I didn't hear from him all week. It turned out that he hadn't returned to his job, but took a few days off and went to Jekyll Island, one of his favorite places in Georgia, to think and to play putt-putt golf.

While he was there, the darkness lifted. One minute it was there and the next minute it wasn't, just like that, just like dawn.

Barry called on a Sunday morning to say that he didn't fully understand what had happened, but that he felt like he had come back, although he wasn't sure if it would be permanent or only temporary.

During the weeks that followed, as the seaweed from around our heads began to untangle and we were able to breathe again and see light, we talked often. He came home often, and we loved each other well.

It was a tender, precious, vulnerable time.

We drove to our favorite neighborhood, the one we used to go to and walk through the houses that were under construction and imagine that the houses belonged to us. During one trip, Barry told me to pick out the lot that I liked, that we would make a down payment and build something just for the two of us.

And so we did.

It may sound hokey, but to me, building our house was a sign from God that He had done what He needed to do and that that particular time of darkness was over.

*For those who are His, God promises an other side, if not in this life, then in eternity.*

I know full well that there are no guarantees of happily ever after this side of heaven. There's mostly toil and hardship, confusion, doubt—and darkness. But there are also enough dawns to let us know that God still is and always will be sovereign and all-mighty.

He sends storms and He sends fish to swallow wayward

prophets and He sends darkness to swallow even His own.

After three days inside the fish, Jonah was vomited out onto the beach, alive.

For those who are His, God promises an other side, if not in this life, then in eternity. And even if it doesn't look like it at times, He is God and He is good. He cannot be anything else.

# Think on These Things

*Think:* When was the last time you questioned if God really was in control? What questions did you have? Do you think people have more difficulty believing in God's power or His goodness? Why do you think that?

*Study:* True rest for the Christian comes in knowing that God is at the same time all-powerful, all-wise, all-knowing, and all-good. What does the Bible say about…

- How well does God know you? (Read Psalm 139; Matthew 10:29–31; and John 1:47–49; 4:1–18.) What are some other Scriptures about God's intimate knowledge of you?
- How much does God love you? (Ephesians 3:17–20; John 3:16; Luke 23:33–34; Romans 8:35–39; Hebrews 13:5; 1 John 3:1.) These are just a few of the many Scriptures about God's love for you.
- How powerful is God? (Genesis 1; Jeremiah 32:17; Ephesians 1:19–21.) For "extra credit," read the confrontation between the ancient Job and God after Job lost his wealth, his children, his health—everything but his nagging wife—and he asked God to explain Himself.

*Apply:* Theologians call the "problem" of God allowing evil in the world a "theodicy." When bad things happen, what do people say about God? How can we discern between truth and fallacy in what people say?

Using the Bible as your reference, list what you know is true about God's sovereignty and providence, and tuck these truths away so you can refer to them when times of darkness come.

*Consider:* In William Cowper's hymn "God Moves in a Mysterious Way," he writes, "Judge not the Lord by feeble sense, But trust Him for His grace; Behind a frowning providence He hides a smiling face."

In tragedy, there is often great good that comes from it. How have you seen God's "smiling face" behind His "frowning providence"?

*Meditate:* "There is no attribute more comforting to His children than that of God's sovereignty. Under the most adverse circumstances, in the most severe trials, they believe that sovereignty has ordained their afflictions, that sovereignty overrules them, and that sovereignty will sanctify them all. There is nothing for which the children ought to more earnestly contend to than the doctrine of their Master over all creation—the Kingship of God over all the works of His own hands—the Throne of God and His right to sit upon that throne…for it is God upon the Throne whom we trust." —Charles Spurgeon

# Chapter Seven

# Ghosts in the Closet

When you're haunted by unforgiveness

*A taste of grace heals an unforgiving heart.*

Carol McGalliard, "Stunned by Grace,"

*Discipleship Journal*

A friend of mine lives with a ghost in her closet.

It's not a real ghost, like those wisps of white or the transparent images of people who supposedly died centuries ago and now their spirits inhabit old hotels in New England and that people hope to see if they stay there overnight.

If it were that kind of a ghost, she could invite her pastor over and they could pray "in Jesus' name" and maybe it would leave.

Actually, my friend wishes it were that kind of a ghost, because then she might be able to get rid of it. But it's not that kind. Hers is a ghost of unforgiveness that lives in her closet and has for more than twenty years, almost all of her married life. It comes out every so often, usually without warning, to haunt and torment her.

As my friend has explained it, when she and her husband had only been married a few years, something happened. She had been, as she calls it, wild and stupid when she was younger. She was driven by a need for love, and since sex usually got her at least a counterfeit version of love, she didn't abstain from it.

After she met and married her husband, she still didn't feel loved, and she met someone who flirted with her. Going into her default mode, she flirted back.

She was young, she said, and didn't understand the complexities and insecurities of the male ego, and although she never did more than flirt with the other guy, it was enough to send her husband into a tailspin.

Without meaning to or realizing it, she had emasculated him. When he confronted her—his mind already made up that she had cheated on him—she retaliated with some hurtful words that further wounded him. He felt castrated and has never fully recovered from it. He tucked the hurt away and put the ghost inside a closet in their marriage, letting it out every now and then to wreak havoc.

My friend said that over the years the ghost has gotten bigger, that maybe her husband feeds it, slips it Pop-Tarts and string cheese under the door. More likely, she said, it's Jack Daniels that gets the ghost to come out.

She said sometimes she will hear the ghost rattling around, like when her husband starts talking in general about people who cheat on their spouses. Ironically, her husband has cheated on her, but the ghost has him convinced that what he did, while not okay, is somehow justified.

My friend said that when her husband starts remembering and visiting old hurts and flings the closet door wide open, when his face turns hard and his words turn accusatory and foul, she sits in silence, trying to will herself invisible, praying that the ghost will go away once and for all.

But her prayers haven't been answered. The ghost hasn't gone away and won't go away, not yet anyway, because it's not up to her to get it to leave. Only her husband can do that.

"I love you," he tells her all the time. But when the ghost comes out, he adds, "But this one thing I will never forgive."

My friend said she lives tenuously. The ghost has stayed in the closet for sometimes several years without so much as a jiggling of the door handle. But sometimes it comes out every few months.

It's been haunting a lot lately, my friend said, and she's feeling fragile and on edge.

"I know how I used to be, but I also know how much Jesus has changed me since I was that young, stupid girl back then," she said. "So if God has forgiven me, why can't my husband forgive me, especially since he did worse things than I did?"

> *"I love you," he tells her all the time.*
> *But when the ghost comes out he adds,*
> *"But this one thing I will never forgive."*

Once I asked her about that, about how she feels and whether or not she's forgiven him.

"Ohmygoodness," she said. "I remember the first time he told me he had something to 'confess.' As he told me what happened, I felt such incredible compassion for him. It might've been different if he had said he was in love with someone else, but I knew this was just a one-time thing. I knew he felt awful; I knew he regretted it and was truly sorry.

"I also knew that I had forgiven him even before he got the first 'I'm sorry' out," she said. "It had to be a God thing—I don't know how else to explain it."

She admitted that she cried after that. It wasn't okay, and it hurt deeply, but she didn't let it become a ghost. Not even when the same thing happened a year later.

"It's amazing how much forgiveness you can have for others when you realize how much you have been forgiven," she said.

I nodded as if I agreed with her because what she said is biblical, and therefore, I couldn't tell her she was a fruitcake. But for the longest time I would replay her words, turning them over in my brain.

> *"It's amazing how much forgiveness you can have for others when you realize how much you have been forgiven," she said.*

On the one hand, this ghost in her closet is a constant source of heartache for her because she never knows when it will slip out of its prison to haunt her. So she's always on guard, keeping a watchful eye on conversations with her husband that might potentially be ghost fodder. She said if she knew what triggered the hauntings, maybe she could avoid them, but there's no set pattern. No rhyme or reason, especially no reason.

It's a terrible way to live. When she talks about this ghost, it's as if her insides are being twisted. She holds her stomach like she's in pain—and she is. Being the target of someone's unforgiveness is quite painful.

So she lives with this ghost and feels punished for something she didn't do and yet appears to hold no resentment for what her husband *did* do. As best as I can tell, she's telling me the truth, and it makes me wonder what I would do if I were her. It makes me wonder why God doesn't smack her husband upside the head. But then, we're all pretty much blind to the depth of our own sin until God opens our eyes.

## Forgiven in the "Low" Places

My friend said, "It's amazing how much forgiveness you can have for others when you realize how much you have been forgiven." A few years ago I asked her if she had been a serial ax murderer or an international jewel thief before she moved to Florida. You never know about people, and the way she talked about being forgiven, I thought she must have had a rap sheet a mile long.

But unless she's a really good liar, her life has been mostly respectable. No prison record or warrants out for her arrest, although she got a speeding ticket once. Actually, she's pretty much a Goody Two-shoes, so I just figured she was neurotic.

> *But then, we're all pretty much blind to the depth of our own sin until God opens our eyes.*

She pulled out her Bible and opened it to the gospel words of Jesus, that we must forgive each other from the heart (Matthew 18:35, my paraphrase), and the words of the apostle Paul, that we are to forgive others just as Christ has forgiven us (Colossians 3:13, my paraphrase).

Once again I nodded. *Yeah, yeah. Sounds good. I believe it says that.*

It took a while until I fully got it, but something happened to make me understand exactly what she meant by realizing how much we've been forgiven in Christ.

For me, it happened at a time when I was feeling particularly good about myself. Not as good as Mother Teresa, but way better than Jeffrey Dahmer or Charles Manson—probably even better than you, if you want to know the truth.

But wouldn't you know, just when I think I'm so far beyond doing something horrendous and outright wrong, I do it.

I stole a packet of Sweet'N Low.

It was just one, and I put it back because I felt guilty. Actually, I put it back because my daughter Laura caught me, and then I felt guilty. But putting it back doesn't change the fact that I am and always will be a Sweet'N Low thief.

*Wouldn't you know, just when I think I'm so far beyond doing something horrendous and outright wrong, I do it.*

Laura and I had been out shopping and stopped for lunch, and even though it was just one tiny packet that was free for restaurant customers who order ice tea or coffee, I hadn't ordered either; I ordered water. I pocketed the packet of Sweet'N Low for my morning coffee the next day because I had run out at home. Even though I had money to buy a box at the market on the way home, I didn't feel like stopping at the store.

Laziness led to my thievery.

So there I was, waiting for my Maui Teriyaki Chicken with the evidence of my sin nature in my pocket. I would've gotten away with it, too, my conscience calling me a sweetener thief the rest of my life notwithstanding. However, my little rat fink of a daughter saw me do it.

"What are you doing?" she yelled, from across the restaurant no less.

It was the kind of question that God asks when He's about to nail you. He doesn't ask because He doesn't know what you're up to. He asks because He wants to make sure *you* know.

Sometimes He uses your kids to do His asking for Him.

"What?" I answered. At times like that I am at my most eloquent.

Then she started yelling, "Mom! You're stealing Sweet'N Low! I can't believe you're stealing Sweet'N Low! *My mom*—the Christian writer—is stealing Sweet'N Low!"

For the hearing impaired, she flashed her accusation across the restaurant in neon lights.

*There I was, waiting for my Maui Teriyaki Chicken with the evidence of my sin nature in my pocket.*

I shrugged. After all, everybody does it, I reasoned.

But it's difficult to fake nonchalance when your kid is lecturing you about your sin in front of an audience of people poised with their forks in midbite. I pictured a SWAT team busting through the door to haul me off to the pokey, where I would be forced to wear stripes and pick up trash with a roadside chain gang.

So I put the packet of Sweet'N Low back. I wouldn't have enjoyed it anyway.

Later at home, as I nursed my humiliation, I started thinking about my sin—about little lies, wasting time at work, forgetting on purpose to make a phone call for my husband, hiding a credit card purchase. Not doing good when it's in my power to do so, ignoring a need, choosing a lesser thing to comfort me rather than turning first to God.

Stealing one tiny, measly packet of Sweet'N Low.

I've never killed anyone, but I've been angry. I've never robbed a bank, but I once took a hymnal home from church and kept it for three years on my bookshelf before returning it.

As I thought about all these seemingly little, insignificant sins—sinlets, if there is such a thing—I realized how great they truly are.

Think about it: He was crucified for my laziness, for my carelessness, for my listening to gossip, for my delighting in evil.

Maybe if I had been a serial killer and Christ offered Himself as a sacrifice for my crimes, at least that would make some sense. But Christ having to die because of one small pink packet of artificial sweetener that I put in my pocket? How much more heinous could that be?

> *Maybe if I had been a serial killer and Christ offered Himself as a sacrifice for my crimes, at least that would make some sense.*

For the first time I realized maybe not the full extent of the forgiveness of God in Christ, but enough so that I understood the seriousness of sin and a tiny bit of the magnitude of God's grace and mercy and love for His own.

Immediately I called my friend and shouted into the phone, "I stole Sweet'N Low!"

I had been forgiven much.


## The Sin of Being Good

I already told you one of my favorite stories that Jesus told His disciples, the one about the runaway son who squanders his inheritance, then returns home expecting to be greeted by a harsh father who rejects him, or at least demands restitution.

To recap: When he sees his father running toward him, and even before he has a chance to beg his father's forgiveness, or even to catch his breath, his father grabs him, hugs him, and kisses him. By this time, they're both sobbing, and the father calls for a huge party to celebrate.

That's the part of the story that most people focus on—the "bad" son being welcomed by the father and restored to the family. It's a picture of God lavishing His grace on those who least deserve it, like you and me.

The story doesn't end there, however. It ends with an older brother, one who does everything right on the outside, but seethes with envy and self-righteousness on the inside and is appalled and disgusted that his father would welcome his loser brother back into the family without even a suggestion of a repayment schedule or a probationary period.

Despite the father's plea to join the party and celebrate, the older brother stays away, sulking.

*After all I've done for the old man…I've always known that he favored that worthless piece of trash brother of mine.… It's not fair—I deserve better.… He's never thrown me a party.… Both of them— they're going to pay for this.… I'm going to get mine, and they're going to get theirs if it's the last thing I do.*

> *Despite the father's plea to join the party and celebrate, the older brother stays away, sulking.*

He hates the father's forgiveness and grace, and can't even see his own sin of "rightness" as he puts this ghost of bitterness and resentment inside his closet. (Luke 15:11–32, my paraphrase)

In the end, which son is enjoying the father's smile?

My pastor, who calls himself a recovering older brother, says that it's much easier for those like the younger brother in the story to find forgiveness and, therefore, offer it, than it is for older brothers. Not that God doesn't offer it to older brothers, but they tend to not think they need it. Or as my husband says, they think their breath doesn't stink.

But unless you know your breath stinks, unless you know the magnitude of your sin and how desperately you need forgiveness, you will never be able to fully appreciate the height and breadth and depth and the greatness of God's mercy. Those who don't know such mercy are the ones who tend to put ghosts in closets and keep them there.

## Sinning Boldly

I got an e-mail once from a reader of my weekly column, a fifteen-year-old obedient virgin—not that there's anything wrong with that. She had taken me to task about something I had written about the grace of God and questioned my salvation. Then she extolled her virtues, listing extensively the areas of her obedience.

I wanted to e-mail her back and tell her to go out and get some real sinning experience and then get back to me.

Martin Luther, in a letter to Philip Melanchthon in 1521, wrote, "If you are a preacher of grace, then preach a true and not a fictitious grace; if grace is true, you must bear a true and not a fictitious sin. God does not save people who are only fictitious sinners. Be a sinner and sin boldly, but believe and rejoice in Christ even more boldly, for He is victorious over sin, death, and the world."

Not that I would ever advocate sinning, and I don't think Martin Luther is doing that here either. My point is that we all sin, grievously, and it makes me crazy to be chastised by someone who thinks she doesn't.

*There is great joy and freedom in knowing the depth of your sin and the even greater depth of God's forgiveness.*

My uncle-dad says that he almost loves to sin because he loves to repent and experience God's forgiveness. Of course, he also says that if I ever tell anyone he says that, he'll deny it.

But I know what he means. One of my favorite Scriptures is 1 John 1:9—"If we confess our sins, he [God] is faithful and just and will forgive us our sins and purify us from all unrighteousness."

John goes on to write, "If we claim we have not sinned, we make him [God] out to be a liar and his word has no place in our lives" (v. 10).

King David once wrote, "Blessed is he whose transgressions are forgiven, whose sins are covered" (Psalm 32:1). There is great joy and freedom in knowing the depth of your sin and the even greater depth of God's forgiveness.

## Revisiting the Ghost

But what do you do with ghosts in your closet?

If they are somebody else's ghosts, like the one my friend wrestles with, there probably isn't a whole lot you can do except not let them destroy you. If you've confessed your sin, then God, who is faithful and just, has forgiven you and purified you from all unrighteousness, and He doesn't hold it against you any longer.

So, you hold on to that. You grasp it, squeeze it tight, own it, let it bring you peace. People accused Jesus all the time of stuff He didn't do, and He never hurled accusations back at His accusers. He knew the truth and didn't need to defend Himself.

But what if you're the one who put the ghosts there? What if you're the one who has been hurt? What if the sins committed against you are unspeakably horrendous?

What if everyone around you tells you that you are justified to harbor these ghosts, that your wounds give you the right to your resentment and bitterness?

In a *Christianity Today* article, psychologist Lewis Smedes wrote that no one really forgives unless he has been hurt, the kind of hurt that is both deep and moral. "Deep because they slice the fiber that holds us together in a human relationship," he wrote. "Moral because they are wrongful, unfair, intolerable. We cannot indulge them or ignore them; we cannot shrug them off. We cannot just chalk them up to the human condition. The sorts of hurts that need forgiving are the ones that tend, in the nature of the case, to build a wall between the wrongdoer and the person he wrongfully hurts."

This is not the hurt of a forgotten lunch date, but of the willful and systematic and purposeful destruction of your person, the damage to your psyche, the wounding of your soul beyond human repair.

> *What if everyone around you tells you that you are justified to harbor these ghosts, that your wounds give you the right to your resentment and bitterness?*

Here's where I risk being heartless, tactless, and flip—and I've done it before with people, so I know what I'm talking about. I can quote you Scripture and tell you that the Bible says to forgive so you have to do it, but I would be guilty of heaping more abuse on you.

Sometimes well-meaning, Bible-wielding people wanting to help don't help at all. Those of us who have never encountered any kind of abuse or evil done to us just want everyone to live happily ever after, singing in the sunshine, dancing in the rain, sitting by the campfire singing "Kumbaya."

But I've met too many women in the past few years who are deeply wounded, carrying around jailers' key rings with keys to closets where their ghosts, their memories, are alive and well and being fed daily. You can't just toss these women a few Scripture verses, yank away their key rings, and tell them to get over it. However, neither can you look the other way as they continue to feed their ghosts—not if you love them.

It's terribly difficult for us humans to forgive. I will even say it's impossible, except that with God all things are possible and nothing is impossible with Him. Therefore, since God has said we must forgive others just as in Christ He has forgiven us, and since when He issues a command He also makes a way for us to follow it, then forgiveness is possible.

> It's terribly difficult for us humans to forgive. I will even say it's impossible, except that with God all things are possible and nothing is impossible with Him.

But how? And what do you do with all the hurt and bitterness and memories? Pretend like nothing ever happened? Sweep it under the rug? Wave it off like it's no big deal?

## Forgiving Grace, Amazing Grace

In my church's Reformed theological tradition, we say that everything is a gift from God. We believe that even repentance and our very faith is a gift from Him to which we respond.

The ability to forgive is also a gift, an act of grace. You can't drum up grace or work for it. You certainly can't deserve it—it just is. God gives it; you receive it.

That's how it is with forgiving those who trespass against us, as it says in the Lord's Prayer. For those great trespasses that are humanly unforgivable, God graces us with the ability to forgive. It can't be any other way, at least that's what I think.

But even though you can't work for grace, you can ask for it. You can even pound on the door of heaven and tell God how much you don't want to forgive, but because it's making your life hell on earth and you hate yourself and everyone around you, you want to at least want to—and would He please give you the grace to do it?

You could do that, and God could answer. I can't promise that He will or that He will answer you right away, but I bet it turns out that He's the One who prompts you to ask in the first place—and if you are His, what He starts in you He always finishes.

*Even though you can't work for grace, you can ask for it.*

So if He starts a work of forgiveness in you, one of these days you will find yourself opening up that closet and telling that ghost to get lost, and you'll be surprised at how puny that ghost really is in comparison to God's great grace.

Smedes wrote, "When you release the wrongdoer from the wrong, you cut a malignant tumor out of your inner life. You set a prisoner free, but you discover that the real prisoner was yourself."

❦

One day a woman came to see me at the newspaper where I work, grinning like a kid on Christmas. As she spilled out in great detail about how her dad had beaten her and her mother and how she had run away and how she had been a bully in school and beat up other kids, the grin never left her face.

Thinking she was not quite right, as I was about to signal to someone in the newsroom to rescue me, she got to the point. Thirty years after the man she had feared and hated died—she hadn't even gone to his funeral, she was so filled with hate—she had finally gone to visit his grave.

"When I got there, I started crying," she said. "A calm came over me, and I said, 'Dad, I forgive you for beating me.'"

That's when she let her ghost out of the closet.

She told me, "My dad was dead all these years, but so was I. I had locked myself up, more interested in surviving than in living, but now I've come alive."

Her grin was contagious, and I grinned, too.

Forgiveness, receiving it and giving it away, will do that to you.

# *Think on These Things*

*Think:* How easy/difficult is it for you to forgive others? Be honest—are there limits to your forgiveness? How do you know if/when true forgiveness has taken place?

*Study:* What does the Bible say about forgiveness and bitterness? To get you started, here are some Scripture references. As you look them up, ask God to show you how His words can heal an unforgiving heart.

Matthew 6:12; 18:21–35; Ephesians 4:32; Colossians 3:13; Hebrews 12:15. What other Scriptures can you find?

*Apply:* The Bible is rich with examples of God forgiving His people. Read the story of the two sons in Luke 15:11–32. Be creative and rewrite or retell it from three different points of view: the runaway son, the waiting father, and the older brother. How does each character in the story perceive forgiveness?

*Consider:* How much have you been forgiven? In light of that, how should you live? (See Luke 15:23–24; Galatians 5:13–15; 6:1–3.)

*Meditate:* "Our first task is not to forgive, but to learn to be the forgiven." — Stanley Hauerwas, *The Peaceable Kingdom*

# Losing Weight, the Jesus Show, and a Twirly White Skirt

### When you're seduced by self

*Most spiritual growth starts with a dose of truth
interfering with a grandiose ego.*
LOUIS TARTAGLIA, MD, *FLAWLESS*

When you're fat all your life and then one day you're not, because you're a sinner (albeit a sinner saved by grace), being no longer fat does strange things to your soul. Of course, so does being fat, but the no longer fat is more dangerous, soul-wise. At least that's how I see it.

I grew up fat. Never to the point of having people stare and point at me on the street, but fat enough to have well-meaning people say, "Such a pretty face, if only she would lose twenty pounds."

Actually, no one ever said that to me, except maybe my mother, but that's what mothers do. We all mean well, most of us anyway, as we proceed to screw up our kids. That's why we all need tons of mercy and grace and forgiveness from God.

By the time I had reached my forties, middle-age spread had done just that. Here's a one-liner I like to tell when I speak at women's events: "The older you get, the tougher it is to lose weight because by then, your body and your fat are really good friends."

That always gets a laugh, but it's not funny. Not if you're fat.

A few years ago, I realized I had spread almost enough to graduate into the plus-size clothing department. Not quite, but almost. At just under five-foot-one, I was a perfect size fourteen petite and shaped perfectly like a beach ball.

I had become good at hiding both my eating and my fat, and I suppose I could have continued like that forever, but I didn't. It was the beginning of January and I had gone to the doctor's for my annual checkup, and he said, "Well, lots of people put on weight as they get older."

I remember thinking, *That's the nicest way anybody has ever told me that I was too fat.* I could tell that my doctor cared about me, about my health, and he told me the same truth then as he had every year: I needed to lose weight. He gave me a certificate for a paid registration to Weight Watchers, and I went to a meeting, joined a gym, and that was that.

> *I had become good at hiding both my eating and my fat, and I suppose I could have continued like that forever, but I didn't.*

In about a year's time I had lost thirty-seven pounds and as many inches, and by the time I turned fifty I had reached my goal.

Because I have vowed to tell you the truth, I have to confess that my goal had nothing to do with pounds and/or inches lost, nor was it my goal to improve my health. My goal—I am almost ashamed to admit this—was to be a hottie. I wanted to turn heads.

At the time I didn't know that was my goal. Some things you only know in retrospect, especially when it involves the corruptness of your own heart.

Through the prophet Jeremiah, God says, "The heart is deceitful above all things and beyond cure. Who can understand it?" (Jeremiah 17:9). The human heart is desperately wicked, perverse, and corrupt, severely, mortally sick—and that's being kind.

No one likes to think of him- or herself as corrupt and wicked, so I told myself feel-good truthful lies like, "Losing weight is good for your health." Technically true, but not soul-fully true. The soul-truth is too confrontational: "You want to lose weight so people will notice you and like what they see."

*My goal—I am almost ashamed to admit this— was to be a hottie. I wanted to turn heads.*

I said that I didn't know that was my goal, but maybe I did. I think you basically know when your thoughts are sin-tinged, but whether you admit it, that's another thing altogether.

So I lost weight, and my daughter Laura bought me a key chain that says "Hottie." I went shopping and bought all new clothes. Nothing revealing, although there's a fine line between what you know is morally right and what you know is borderline morally wrong, and I would buy and wear things that teetered on the edge of that line without actually crossing over it, which probably meant I had crossed over. No, not probably—for me, I had definitely crossed over because it's a heart issue, not a low-cut T-shirt or snug-fit jeans issue.

Then one time Laura and I were in a store, and she said,

"Mom—that guy over there is totally checking you out!"

My brain clicked just then, and I went into an even deeper dive into self-absorption, self-exaltation, and all the other self-words. I had crossed over from being mildly, annoyingly obsessive in my newfound hotness to becoming vainglorious, glorying in my own excessive vanity.

And it seeped out into other parts of my life, parts that had nothing to do with having been fat and getting thin and becoming a total hottie.

I had attended a seminar at my church where the speaker, the Rev. Fred Harrell, pastor of City Church in San Francisco, talked about the counterintuitive way of doing church. He talked about the old-fashioned way of doing church with its religious jargon and finger-pointing "us versus them" mentality toward those outside the church and contrasted it with the new way some churches are adopting. These cool churches (my description) are adjusting their language while maintaining the purity and integrity of the message, thus creating a seeker-comprehensible church environment, immersing themselves in the culture and not isolating themselves from it.

I left the seminar excited—about his church, about my church. He had said that my church was a model for the new style, for "seeker-comprehensible," which meant I was a part of this innovative, cool thing that God is doing. Plus, I looked good. Could life be any greater?

> *My brain clicked just then and I went into an even deeper dive into self-absorption, self-exaltation, and all the other self- words.*

If I were God, I would have zapped me with a lightning bolt or smote me with boils just about then. Better than that, I would have given me a disease or syndrome that needed steroid shots that would have made me gain back all the weight I lost plus fifty or sixty pounds. If I were God, I would have shouted at me to stop and warned me that I was headed for a fall.

On second thought, maybe He did do that and I just didn't hear him.


## What the Mirror Knows

When I was fat I hated mirrors, but when I got thin I loved them. I loved them so much that I made mental notes of the most flattering ones within a forty-mile radius (visiting them often) and which ones to avoid.

You can do that with the Word of God, too. In many ways the Bible is like a mirror, reflecting who you really are, which isn't flattering. However, you can train yourself to look only at the pages and passages where you look best. I'm good at that. I'm good at not seeing my flaws and imperfections and thinking they look better than they are.

> *When I became thin, I became like a bald man with a bad comb-over, only worse.*

However, that's like being a bald man with a bad comb-over. He may think he looks great. He may even convince himself that he, indeed, has a full head of hair and that when women smile at him, they're smiling because they want to run their fingers through it. But he's only fooling himself. He's still billiard cue b-a-l-d, and everyone knows it but him.

When I became thin, I became like a bald man with a bad comb-over, only worse. My newspaper columns took a turn from being God-glorying to being 100 percent me-glorying.

Actually, it was less of a turn than it was a gradual shifting. It's like when you're at the beach, floating on a raft in the gulf waters, not really paying attention to anything other than how good the sun feels on your skin, and you look up and realize the tiny speck on the sand way down the beach is your dad waving to you and calling you. That you've drifted too far and it's time to come back.

Recently, I filled out a test called "How Do You Know If Your Self-Regard Has Run Riot?" found in the book *Flawless* by Louis Tartaglia, MD. Among the questions, it asked:

1. Are you one of the chosen few who should have more say in how the world is run?
2. Do you justify selfish behavior with the rationalization that you are taking care of yourself?
3. Do you believe that everyone should—or better yet would— like you?
4. Are you so self-absorbed that you think self-regard is self-esteem?
5. Do you think you always have the best of intentions even when you do things that are wrong?
6. When people ask how you are, do you give them a really long answer and think it's interesting?
7. Do you spend a lot of time before a mirror and is that where you have your most intense conversations?

It shouldn't surprise anyone that I went seven for seven, answering yes to all of them—and those are just the questions I'm telling you about. There were about a dozen more on the test. However, I took the test long after my newspaper columns made that shift from being God-glorying to being just me-glorying.

I had started writing in my column all about the clothes I was wearing and how I felt about myself now that I was no longer fat, blah, blah, blah, etc., ad nauseam.

After a while I got an e-mail from an editor at a paper in Indiana who passed on some reader criticism: "She certainly is stuck on herself."

That stung, but not enough for God to get my attention, if that was intended to be a message from Him and not just some snarky comment from some cranky-pants reader in Indiana.

> *Truly, the only sufficient remedy for such imagined character assassination, especially when you're no longer fat, is a trip to Macy's.*

I thought about it for maybe all of a minute and a half, then hit Reply and wrote the editor a list of woes and excuses about how I had been fat all my life and now I'm not and I'm just learning to enjoy my new set of skin, more blah blah, more etcetera, definitely more ad nauseam. I may have even accused him of being mean and that his readers were ignorant hayseeds.

In a moment of sanity or clarity, or maybe it was God deciding to be merciful to His waywardly self-absorbed child, I didn't send the e-mail, although I continued to be greatly offended. Misunderstood and maligned. I even added "persecuted for my faith" to my mental list of reasons for this perceived attack.

Truly, the only sufficient remedy for such imagined character assassination, especially when you're no longer fat, is a trip to Macy's. Besides, I needed something to wear to an upcoming wedding. That started a series of things happening that caused me to end up on my face before God, which is, truthfully, the best place one can be. It's just painful getting there.

## A Twirly White Skirt

As I headed to Macy's, it occurred to me that I had fallen head over heels in love with myself. No, I take that back. I didn't realize it, and that was the problem. I should have, but I didn't. I was too busy searching for the ideal wedding guest outfit and looking for flattering mirrors so I could reassure myself that I hadn't lost any of my newfound hotness. I ended up buying a twirly white skirt, and then went home and wrote a column about it, detailing how perfectly it fit and how great it looked.

> *As I headed to Macy's, it occurred to me that I had fallen head over heels in love with myself.*

Yeah, I know. Self-regard run riot. I know that now, and I'm thoroughly embarrassed by it, but back then I didn't see it. It gets worse, too.

To spiritualize my whole twirly white skirt column, I inserted a story Jesus once told a crowd of people about what to wear to a wedding. This is what I wrote:

Jesus told the people that the kingdom of God was like a man who gave a huge wedding for his son. However, the guests he had originally invited didn't want to attend, so the father sent his servants out to invite anyone and everyone, even beggars and thieves. They came, dined on caviar, fancy crudités, and fine wine and had a great time.

But then the father noticed one guest who had slipped in without wearing the proper clothes. In those days it was the custom in the East for the party host to provide guests with festal garments.

No garment—no entry.

Next, the bouncer at the door was told to boot the man out and not let him back in. This is the famous "weeping and wailing and gnashing of teeth" Bible passage (which confirms my belief that not wearing the right outfit is hell).

Jesus went on to make this point about the kingdom of heaven: "Many are called, but few are chosen" (Matthew 22:1–14, paraphrase mine).

Who, then, are the ones who are chosen to enter heaven? The ones who are dressed properly. But unlike even the most perfect twirly white skirt, the proper wedding attire Jesus was talking about is the garment provided by the Father, through faith in the Son. The Bible calls this garment the "righteousness of Christ."

Without it, we can't even make it past the bouncer at the door. With it, even thieves and beggars get in. It's always a perfect fit, never out of fashion, and looks great with or without sandals.

Back then, I thought that was probably the single most clever column I had ever written, which makes me want to retch just thinking about my massive ego gone amok.


## A True Love Story

Before I tell you about the next thing that happened, let me tell you about Narcissus, a gorgeous, Brad Pitt–like creature in Greek mythology who one day knelt by a pool of water to get a drink and saw his own reflection. Thinking it was some beautiful water spirit living in the fountain, he fell in love with the "bright eyes, those locks curled like the locks of Bacchus or Apollo, the rounded cheeks, the ivory neck, the parted lips, and the glow of health all over."

He had fallen in love with himself.

As he came closer for a kiss, he plunged his arms into the water for an embrace, only to see his beloved disappear. Dumb as rocks—and madly in love—he waited until the beautiful creature returned, and he continued this love pursuit for days, unable to tear himself away from the sight of his own image. Eventually, he pined away and died.

What a dope. If that's not self-regard run riot, nothing is, unless you count the next thing that happened to me.

It happened as I began sharing my "self-in-love-ness" with my husband, giving him daily updates of the latest compliment received, who gave it, and my reply. The day my twirly skirt column was printed in the paper, I had followed him around the house reading it to him, completely enamored with myself.

*Back then, I thought that was probably the single most clever column I had ever written, which makes me want to retch just thinking about my massive ego gone amok.*

Because he either (a) loves me, (b) got fed up, or (c) both, he firmly told me that (a) I was in love with myself and (b) to keep it to myself.

In retrospect, it was loving of him to point out my sin, but I didn't think so at the time. At the time, I was just ticked. So, grabbing my "Hottie" key chain, I muttered under my breath, "I'm glad you're not a mind reader," and took off for the gym.

# The Jesus Show

It's been my experience that when God sets out to teach a person something, He's not going to waste His time, and He sets situations in motion so the person gets the complete lesson and not the CliffsNotes version. Plus, He goes for the root of the problem, not just the symptoms.

For me, the whole weight loss/in-love-ness with myself was only part of a deeper problem.

Beauty, as they say, is only skin deep, but ugly goes to the bone. Pride—self-regard run riot—goes deeper than even bone-deep ugly. At fifty, I may look better than I ever have, but God sees past that to the ugly within.

> *It's been my experience that when God sets out to teach a person something, He's not going to waste His time.*

I had left my house in a huff and headed to the gym, but I never made it there. Instead, I took a detour to the downtown area of my city, which is a short, one-way street that ends at the courthouse. Still smarting from my husband's remarks, I sat down on a bench to stew a while. That's when the final thing began—the Jesus Show. That's what a friend calls the street preachers who come like clockwork to the sidewalk in front of the courthouse every Saturday afternoon. They hold signs that say things like "Repent!" and "The wages of sin is death!"

They're often joined by women dressed in plain clothing and no makeup who walk down the street passing out gospel tracts and asking people, "If you were to die tonight, do you know for certain that you would go to heaven?" as the main preacher yells a sermon to the people trying to ignore him as they walk down the street.

So as I sat on the bench and watched the Jesus Show setting up, I thought about how, in this *Queer Eye*–MTV–digital–plasma society, these street preachers in their dark slacks, white shirts, and dark ties were *Andy of Mayberry*–nickel ice cream–rotary dial telephone. I had decided, in a smug, self-righteous, blind sort of way, that their old-fashioned methods and their old-timey gospel singing and King James platitudes were ineffective in today's culture.

*They don't know from counterintuitive*, I thought. *They're not part of the cool thing.*

As I sat there, God showed up. I thought maybe He was there to trade snarky comments about the Show and how they're not part of the cool thing, but it turned out that He had other things on His mind. "Honey," He said, "let's chat about pride."

*How ironic*, I thought. Just a few days before a friend from work and I were talking about that very thing. He had given up pride for Lent the year before, and we had laughed about how proud he was to have attempted it and how, since then, he's had a 180-degree change in his thinking about a lot of things, including pride.

That's what self-regard run riot is. It's pride in its purest sense, setting self up as a highest thing, higher even than God, although most folks seldom see it that way. That's the seductive, sneaky, covert power of pride, especially when it looks like humility. Like the woman I met once who said, "When I pray, I *never* ask God for anything; I *only* give thanks."

On the surface that sounds "unprideful," oozing humility. But the way she said it, it oozed pride. It oozed self. Humility depends on asking God for daily bread. Pride says, "Thanks God, but I'll do this myself."

So when God wanted to chat about pride, I was right there

with Him, ready to add my two cents to the conversation, especially about the Jesus Show people. I had decided that it was their pride that kept them stuck in the spiritual Stone Age and that I was glad to be past that and be part of the cool, counterintuitive thing.

*When God wanted to chat about pride, I was right there with Him, ready to add my two cents to the conversation.*

However, I should have known that when God brings up a topic of conversation with you, it's rarely so you can spout your inane babblings. Instead, it's usually so He can point out your sin (and not the sin of others).

As we sat on the bench, God held up a mirror and told me to take a look. In it I saw Narcissus, only it didn't look like Brad Pitt, but like me, a dope in love with her own image, with her own sense of cool, with her own sense of who God can use to further His kingdom.

I saw a woman easily seduced, easily drawn away from God, the King of everything, and to the vainglorious. I was angry that I hadn't seen it coming, but that's the whole slyly treacherous modus operandi of seduction. It starts tiny, with a word, a thought, a glance, a doubt, playing to your weaknesses and your lusts. As it flatters and woos, it makes you feel good, and it's that feeling, that high, that pulls like a narcotic, feeding your all-about-me-ness, which is insatiable.

Eventually you go blind, unless someone comes along who loves you enough to tell you the truth about yourself. Like my doctor had done years earlier, like my husband had done earlier that day.

Like God continues to do.

*I saw a woman easily seduced, easily drawn away from God, the King of everything, and to the vainglorious.*

But—and this is what I love about God—when He sits down and chats with you about your sin, He doesn't leave you in your blindness. He didn't leave me to stew in my sin or even to devise ways to atone for it myself or make me give up pride for Lent. Instead, He reminded me that, "If we confess our sins, he is faithful and just and will forgive us our sins and purify us from all unrighteousness" (1 John 1:9).

So that's what I did, and then I went home to (a) thank my husband for telling me the truth and (b) ask his forgiveness.

Here's where I would like to say, "And ever since, I've never looked in a mirror to check out my appearance or trumpeted myself either in my column or my conversation," but that wouldn't be true. I will always battle self. I am easily seduced.

The best thing I can hope for is that next time I'm tempted to linger in front of my own reflection, I'll remember Narcissus and how it is possible to love yourself to death.

# Think on These Things

*Think:* When you think of a seduction, what words or images come to mind? In our society, what types of things are seductive? Why do you think some people are more easily seduced than others?

*Study:* Some call pride a root sin. Using a dictionary and a thesaurus, list all the definitions and synonyms for pride. Do the same for all the words with the prefix "self" (e.g., self-importance). Look up *pride, proud, humble,* and *humility* in the Bible to see what God says.

*Apply:* Read Luke 18:9–14. Whose prayer most reflects your own? In contrast, Colossians 3:12; Titus 3:2; and 1 Peter 5:5–7 talk about humility. How is humility a strength? Pray and ask God to show you the areas in which you lack humility.

*Consider:* From Eve in the Garden of Eden to you and me in the twenty-first century, even when we are deceived and seduced by pride and fall into sin, God offers absolute forgiveness. Memorize 1 John 1:9 and quote it to yourself often—and believe it!

*Meditate:* "Think about yourself. Talk about yourself. Use 'I' as often as possible. Mirror yourself continually in the opinion of others. Listen greedily to what people say about you. Expect to be appreciated. Be suspicious. Be jealous and envious. Be sensitive to slights. Never forgive a criticism. Trust nobody but yourself. Insist on consideration and respect. Demand agreement with your own views on everything. Sulk if people are not grateful to you for favors shown them. Never forget a service you have rendered. Shirk your duties if you can. Do as little as possible for others." —unknown author, "How to Be Miserable"

# Chapter Nine

# Footwashings and
# a Resurrection
### When your heart is cold

*His life-giving water had tasted dull in my mouth.*
CASSIDY WALL, HIGH SCHOOL STUDENT

I can't pinpoint the moment that I died, nor the moment that I realized I was dead, but somewhere along the way I just knew.

Maybe you know what it's like. You're breathing and moving. Your cheeks are pink; you're a success at your job. You're doing and being. You laugh and sing, enjoy a rowdy game of Scrabble now and then, make a mean tamale pie that causes your family to hoist you on their shoulders and carry you around the house.

People who know you well, and even those who only know you slightly, look at you and think—even say out loud—"You are blessed."

And you know that you are. You know that God has showered His gracious favor and tender mercy on you. You know that your life is unimaginably rich and full.

But you also know that somehow, somewhere—you're not sure when (or maybe you are)—at some point your soul shriveled up like a dust-covered grape that has rolled under the refrigerator and died, and you haven't been able to raise yourself back up.

That's how it is when you're dead. You can't will your life back. All you can do is hope for a resurrection.

Here's the irony of the situation: Even though I had been dead for a while, week after week I had still been able to write my weekly column about God's amazing grace, and I had still been able to speak at women's retreats all about life and what true living is—and mean every word with all my heart.

Preachers do that, too, I'm told. Preachers and Bible teachers and Christian writers and speakers mostly communicate what they know is true and what they want to be true of their own experience, even though sometimes, maybe even often, the two don't match up.

*That's how it is when you're dead.*
*You can't will your life back.*
*All you can do is hope for a resurrection.*

I often tell people that if you want to know what I struggle with, read my books. I've written two on prayer, not because I've mastered the subject, but because I lack woefully. It's the same thing when I write and speak about freedom in Christ. Even though I know it and believe it and can quote the Scriptures that prove it, even though I've tasted it and reveled in it, I don't always live in it. Not all the time anyway, and especially not when I'm living in deadness, which sounds impossible, but I do it all the time. I'm getting quite good at it actually.

# How You Get to Be Dead

As I think back on my soul's deaths (I use the plural because I think it's possible to suffer from chronic death, not just a one-time occurrence, like chicken pox; it's more like the flu), here are some of the symptoms I've experienced:

- A sense that God must surely regret having me as His child.
- Thoughts of—*I need to pray more (and harder). I need to read my Bible more and muster up more love for God's Word. But I don't want to pray and read the Bible. I want to sit on my couch, watch reruns of* Gilmore Girls, *and eat cake."*
- General low-grade feelings of nonspecific guilt and spiritual ickiness.
- Attacks of hypocrisy and feelings of being an imposter or illegitimate, coupled with an acute fear of being exposed as a spiritual fraud.
- Intense, self-imposed isolation. I am a loner by nature; however, there's a fine line between that and not wanting to be around people because they irritate you and their neediness forces you to care about someone other than yourself, and frankly, you just don't want to be bothered.
- A dull sense of homesickness or nostalgia for what once was; a feeling of lostness and of not knowing how to get back; a sense of having gone too far, coupled with a fear of not being able to get back even if you knew how.

Here are some of my thoughts on how one finds him- or herself dead. For some, it's a conscious decision, like the bunny in Margaret Wise Brown's *The Runaway Bunny*, or Max, the "king of the wild things," in Maurice Sendak's *Where the Wild Things Are*, or the youngest son in Jesus' story of the Prodigal Son. Each of them one day decided, "I'm outa here."

That's immediate soul-death, although I need to clarify something. When a true child of God walks away, the child remains a child; the Father remains the Father. The relationship isn't severed, not on God's end anyway, and any feelings of death are experiential or "as if." It's when you say, "My soul might as well be dead because that's how it feels."

## A Wandering Death

Sometimes when you're dead you think you're the only one, but then you meet someone else who has her own soul-death story, and you realize it's common to most everyone.

One of my favorite former-dead-people stories belongs to my friend Crysynda. She's tall, with long, wild, curly red hair, and she's quite Pentecostal. I'm short, with short, spiky brown hair and not even a little bit Pentecostal, but we're friends.

I first met Crysynda when she was the pastor at a tiny local Pentecostal church and I had gone to do a story on her for the newspaper. She said that as a kid, while her friends watched cartoons on TV, she watched Kathryn Kuhlman, Billy Graham, and Oral Roberts. At age nine she knew that God had called her to the deepest, darkest jungles of Africa to preach the Word to the lost.

Although she was wrong about Africa, she did manage to fall into darkness.

*When a true child of God walks away, the child remains a child; the Father remains the Father.*

She left home at eighteen to go to college and change the world for Jesus. She began by marrying a non-Christian, alcoholic, hemophiliac, whom she eventually divorced. Then she became an ordained full-gospel minister and traveled as an evangelist, preaching three services a day, seven days a week, plus doing radio and television. Eventually she burned out and dumped the whole ministry.

She said she had become disillusioned and disgusted at things she saw taking place in the name of God, the corruption and abuse of power by God's ministers. One in particular would tell poor people that unless they gave God their food stamps and jewelry, they couldn't receive a blessing. "It made me so sick to see this that I left everything," she said.

> *She left home at eighteen to go to college and change the world for Jesus. She began by marrying a non-Christian, alcoholic, hemophiliac, whom she eventually divorced.*

Lonely and disillusioned, she started going to bars, singing karaoke, snorting coke. For Crysynda, her soul-death was a conscious decision. *If this is what God is all about, then I don't want any part of it. Adios.*

But for me, and maybe for you, my death was less of a decision to run and more of a wandering away. I wandered to death.

A wandering death is like floating on a raft at the beach. You go in the water and swim out past the breaking waves. You climb onto your raft and let the hot sun and the soft bobbing of the water lull you into a state of not caring about anything else. You can't even open your eyes to see where you are.

But when you eventually do, if a shark hasn't eaten you or a jellyfish hasn't stung you, you're shocked at how far you've drifted.

And depending on how far you are from your blanket on the beach, you might panic or you might decide to stay adrift forever.

When I discovered that I could hardly see God, like He was a teeny dot on the beach, I opted for panicking—I didn't like feeling adrift.

At church, whenever we would sing, "Prone to wander, Lord, I feel it, prone to leave the God I love…" I felt it. I still feel it. It feels panicky, and I would pray the only prayer I could think of: "Jesus, I'm lost! Please find me."

I suppose you could argue the point that if I could pray, I wasn't really dead. So I'll concede that point and just say that I was dead-ish. Potatoes, potahtoes. The point is, I needed God to find me and breathe life into me once again.

And another thing—I don't care what people say; you can follow a checklist of rules and principles and keys until you turn blue, but when you're feeling dead inside, you can't manufacture a desire for God that way. You can't come alive to a strategy or be warmed by a how-to. About all you can do is hold out what little life you have in your hand and hope that God's hand is already there, ready to pull you close.

When you're dead, or deadish, only God can resurrect you. That's just a fact.


## Preaching to the Bones

There's an odd story in the Old Testament book of Ezekiel, chapter 37. God takes Ezekiel, a priest, to a valley that's filled with dry bones. God asks, "Do you think these bones can live?"

"Only you know that," Ezekiel says.

"I want you to speak to these bones and tell them that I will breathe life into them and they will come alive with flesh and tendons and skin—and then they will know that I am the Lord," God says.

So Ezekiel does what God says, and as he's preaching to the bones he hears a rattling sound, and all the bones appear with tendons and flesh and skin, but no breath in them. God tells Ezekiel to "prophesy to the breath," and as he does, breath enters the bones and they come to life and stand up—a vast army of them (vv. 1–10, my paraphrase).

> ⌇ My point in telling you this story is to let you know that breathing life into death is an everyday occurrence to God. ⌇

God goes on to tell Ezekiel that the meaning of that little resurrection exercise has to do with Israel, that the people who were in exile and held captive by the Babylonians had cried out to God, "Our bones are dried up and our hope is gone."

They had drifted far from God, and He had let them feel the dryness of their deadened souls. By showing Ezekiel the army of living bones, God is telling him that He (God) would one day bring the people of Israel back to their homeland and that when He does, when He brings their dusty bones and dry souls to life, they will know that God alone did it.

"I will put my Spirit in you and you will live, and I will settle you in your own land," God tells Ezekiel. "Then you will know that I the Lord have spoken, and I have done it" (v. 14).

My point in telling you this story is to let you know that breathing life into death is an everyday occurrence to God. He does it all the time, although I personally have never seen a skeleton walking around with skin and flesh attached. I have however, seen lots of deadish people who have been brought back to life—like Crysynda.

## Gospel and Coke

As I was telling you, Crysynda had walked away from anything having to do with God or the ministry. She thought Christians and Christianity were pretty much bunk, but not completely. She said something way, way deep within her that wouldn't— couldn't—stop believing. That's one of the reasons she snorted coke. She couldn't reconcile the corruption of Christian ministries she had seen with the deep belief that once made her dance and sing and love Jesus with all her heart.

The cocaine helped her forget, she said. But she couldn't really forget. Once God's Spirit has taken up residence in you, once God has adopted you into the family and Jesus has become your Brother and Friend, you can't ever forget. God won't let you, even if you try.

Crysynda tried. She hooked up with a major cocaine dealer in Michigan and would travel with him to Florida to pick up drug shipments.

"I'm not proud of this," she said, "and I know this isn't what God wanted for my life, but the whole time I was getting high I was still preaching the Word. People would come to me with their spiritual questions, and I'd open the Bible and we'd pray together. I'm not condoning this. It's just how it was."

Some people might think that's sacrilege or hypocrisy, but that's my favorite part of her story. As deadish as she was, as dark as the darkness in which she found herself, she still had a little light inside of her, and God was able to shine through her in a way that someone else might not have been able to with that group of people in that situation.

Doesn't that blow you away? Even when we are far from him, God can and will still use us. No matter how dim our light, it still shines in the darkness. I don't know about you, but that gives me great hope, especially when I feel myself starting to drift.

As for the rest of Crysynda's story, she had been high for five days when she was stopped by the police. She had cocaine all over the seat of her car. Plus, she had a gun with her.

"I was in the backseat of the police car, and I knew that I was in trouble," she said. "But I also knew that God had never left me. While the officer searched my car I begged God for help—and the officer came back and just let me go!"

*No matter how dim our light,
it still shines in the darkness.*

Crysynda didn't make a 180-degree change right then, but that scared her enough to start her thinking seriously about how far she had run from Jesus. She went on to Florida and still used cocaine, but she also started reading her Bible more. Her getting clean was gradual—she started loving Jesus more than she loved coke.

Eventually God called her back into the ministry, after He first called her back to life.

## Dead Man Walking

A few years ago I had been invited to be the speaker at a beach house retreat, right on the white sands of northern Florida's east coast. It was what I call a "suffering for Jesus" weekend—gourmet food, a room to myself overlooking the ocean, and women eager to hear the Word of God. However, I was not all that eager to actually study and read the Word, since I was deep into my death at that time.

To tell you the truth, it had probably been months since I had opened my Bible for anything other than work-related reasons.

Maybe even a year or two. I'm not proud of this, but I feel compelled to tell you like it is.

I was dead, dead, dead.

But I wasn't dead enough to keep from wanting to go to the beach and eat great food and maybe sell some books and earn a few bucks by doing this retreat. Besides, I had given the same set of talks at least two dozen times before and knew I could do them in my sleep, or in my case, my death.

Many times I feel guilty and slimy of soul when I accept an invitation to speak, especially when I'm feeling particularly unholy and unalive, and I always give the person who invites me every opportunity to uninvite me. So far, no one's taken me up on it.

So I go, knowing full well that my light is dim at best and that if God doesn't show up and do something, then all that the women who have come will get is a bunch of dry bones.

That's how it was with the beach house retreat. I knew that I was going not fully alive. I felt like an imposter and a fake, and I begged God not to let me screw it up too badly or say something that would cause the women to throw their shoes at me or walk away from Jesus and become Buddhists.

I don't remember if I had asked God for a resurrection or not. I'm sure that I didn't. I'm not generally in the habit of asking for things like that. But I do remember feeling deader than I had felt in a long time, if that's even possible.

I'm talking dusty bones dead.

❧

Jesus once had a friend named Lazarus who died. When the news came that His friend was sick, Jesus didn't rush to be with him, but stayed where He was. Then after four days, He decided that it was time to head back, since Lazarus had already died.

This is a good place to say that, on the surface, God appears to have terrible timing. He often lets situations get out of hand (in my opinion). He lets folks die, even if He plans to raise them back to life. You would think that He would not let them die in the first place and spare people's grief and all.

But then, you can't have a resurrection without a corpse.

So Jesus gathered His disciples and headed to Lazarus's tomb, and that's where He wept. He is a God who weeps because of death, and I'm hoping that when we're sitting on our couches watching reruns of *Gilmore Girls*, dying inside, He weeps for us as well. And I'd be surprised if He isn't also planning our resurrections then, too.

*You can't have a resurrection without a corpse.*

Next, Jesus called His friend's name: "Lazarus! Come out!" And the once-dead man, after hearing the voice of God, got up and walked out of his grave.

Just like that.

## Welcome to *My* Resurrection

If you asked him, I'm sure that Lazarus could pinpoint the exact moment he heard Jesus calling him back to life; however, I'm not certain of the moment that my resurrection happened. I think it happened as I sat on the beach watching the ocean and God just sort of quietly showed up.

I think that He sat next to me on my towel, and as He pointed out the ocean He had created eons before, He let me know that His love for me was deeper, vaster, broader, wider and that I couldn't run farther than His hand could reach, nor wander out of His sight. I couldn't even build a wall thick enough to keep Him out.

As I listened to the waves crashing and felt the sun warm my skin and amused myself watching a little boy who was trying to ride his bicycle in the sand, God sat with me, reminding me that neither life nor death, neither tiredness nor apathy nor blahness of spirit could ever separate me from His love.

We sat on the beach together, God and I, for what seemed hours, not saying much of anything. Maybe mine was a slow-acting resurrection because nothing really happened that I could tell.

I stayed on the beach until the sun started to set. Later that night, the women had a footwashing. Jesus had told His disciples once that because they were His, they were already clean and didn't need a (ceremonial) bath, but that the everydayness of the journey made their feet dirty.

*Maybe I died from dirty feet*, I thought, but to this day I still don't know.

The night before He died, Jesus washed His disciples' feet, and that night He washed mine.

Normally I tend to freak out at things like footwashings. You can ask my kids—I've been known to kill people who touch my feet. But I allowed Jesus, disguised as two women who had come to the beach house retreat, to wash my feet and pray blessings over me. Afterwards we all ate cookies the size of boulders.

> *Maybe mine was a slow-acting resurrection because nothing really happened that I could tell.*

To tell you the truth, I didn't feel resurrected, but I didn't feel quite as dead. At the time I thought it must have been from all the sugar in the cookies I ate.

But the next morning…

The next morning I danced—and I don't normally dance.

Sometime between sitting on the beach and the footwashing and the speaking words of life to the beach house women and letting strangers love me, sometime between the resting and sleeping late and feasting on good food, at some point I realized I was alive again, that I had been resurrected.

And so I danced.

Crysynda dances, and although I don't know for a fact that that's what Lazarus did, I wouldn't be surprised. That's what a resurrection does to you.

And in case you're wondering—I'm still dancing.

# Think on These Things

*Think:* In *When I Don't Desire God*, author John Piper says that preferring Jesus to anything else is a gift of God. He writes, "We can't produce it on our own. It must be given to us." Do you agree or disagree, and why?

*Study:* The Psalms are filled with emotion, of delighting in and desiring God. Read the following Psalms and note how each addresses the ideas of delight and desire, and also the obstacles or hindrances to desiring God: Psalm 16; 34; 37; 42; and 73.

*Apply:* Write your own psalm, pouring out your honest thoughts, whether they are of passionate desire or lukewarm blahness toward God. Keep writing until it becomes a prayer. (Note how some of the Psalms start with anger or worry or bitterness and end in praise.)

*Consider:* In his hymn "Come, Thou Fount of Every Blessing," Robert Robinson penned the words "Prone to wander, Lord, I feel it, prone to leave the God I love." When your heart starts to wander, consider Jesus, our great Shepherd (Luke 15:3–7; Psalm 23). What comfort do these passages give to a wandering heart?

*Meditate:* "There have been times when I think we do not desire heaven; but more often I find myself wondering whether, in our heart of hearts, we have ever desired anything else." —C. S. Lewis, *The Problem of Pain*

# Chapter Ten

# It's Okay to Be *F.I.N.E.

## (*Fouled-up, Insecure, Neurotic, and Exhausted)

### When you're free to tell the truth

*When you and I stop pretending, we expose the
pretending of everyone else. The bubble of the perfect
Christian life is burst, and we must all face
the reality of our brokenness.*
MICHAEL YACONELLI, *MESSY SPIRITUALITY*

I have decided that I could be a perfect wife if it wasn't for my
husband.

We've been married for more than thirty years, and for seven
of those I actually was as near to perfect as one can get this side
of heaven.

Not all the time, but for most of it.

For seven years my husband worked and, therefore, lived 130
miles away and only came home several times a month. It was
during his away times that, as a wife, I was perfect.

When he wasn't there, I said all the perfect things a wife should
say; I did all the perfect things. I shared perfectly, compromised

and negotiated textbook perfectly. I was perfectly self-sacrificing and self-controlled and all the other good "self" attributes.

It was easy—it was all in my mind. In my mind, I was the perfect wife.

But then last year my husband retired and moved back home, and my perfection blew up in my face. After seven years of having everything the way I like it (meaning, revolving around me), Barry returned and more or less disrupted my status quo.

For the first few weeks it was honeymoonish. I would look at him sitting on the couch or hanging out in the garage, and I'd think, *I can't believe he's back—he's just so cute!* I'd be all smiley and goo-goo eyed.

> *It was easy—it was all in my mind. In my mind, I was the perfect wife.*

Then he declared his edict. He had said, even before he retired, that he only wanted one thing to change. He wanted to get digital cable for the TV.

However, I didn't want digital cable, not that I even understand what digital means. All I knew was that with our nondigital cable I had finally learned how to program the VCR to tape reruns of *Gilmore Girls* while I was at work so I would never have to miss an episode.

Yes, I fully realize how shallow and petty this sounds, but I'm not done yet. It gets worse.

Whenever Barry would mention digital cable, I would roll my eyes and shake my head, as if he had said he wanted to host cockfights in the living room or something equally outrageous. And the whole time I did it, I knew it was wrong of me and I hated doing it, but I kept doing it anyway.

So despite my loud, silent protesting, the cable guy came over one day while I was at work, and I came home to find not one but three remotes, two instruction books, and four pages listing the 11 billion channels we now have to choose from—and that I would have to relearn how to program the VCR.

As it is, I don't understand techno language, so it took me more than an hour playing with the various remotes to figure out that my life as I had known it for the previous seven years had been disrupted and that I now had to share it and my living space 24-7 with someone who doesn't think like I do and who has different interests and opinions and who thinks his ways are equal to (or sometimes better than) mine.

Not only that, I couldn't get the blasted VCR to program, all because of the invasion of the digital cable, which made me snarly and snappish.

I seethed. I wanted my *Gilmore Girls*!

Although I tried not to be snarly and snappish, I was. The depth of my shallowness, that I could become that upset over something so insignificant and petty, horrified me—but not enough to want to do anything about it.

I went to bed fussing and fuming to myself and woke up early the next morning, too early to get up but too late to go back to sleep, which didn't help my mood any. So I planned how I would buy myself a combination TV/VCR to put in the spare room that still only had basic cable, and I would lock myself in and watch *Gilmore Girls* nonstop and only come out to refill my popcorn bucket and use the bathroom.

*Take that, digital cable boy*, I thought as I lay there, plotting and listening to Barry breathe.

*The depth of my shallowness horrified me—but not enough to want to do anything about it.*

That's when Barry stirred. God probably nudged him, that's what I think. And then God nudged me, and I thought about repenting, which is always a good way to start the day.

I don't believe in karma or luck, so that's not why I repented. Like I said, God nudged me, and repentance is almost always His idea in the first place.

So, I put my hand on Barry and prayed all kinds of blessings over him, which nearly killed me because I was still ticked over the digital cable thing.

But a funny thing happens when you pray for someone. You start thinking of good things, and that kind of wrecks your snarliness. It also amplifies *your* not-perfect-ness.

To make matters worse, as a surprise Barry had rigged up a switch so that whenever I want to use the VCR, all I have to do is flip a button and it will revert back to nondigital cable, so life as I had come to know and love will go on.

My husband certainly knows how to ruin a good hissy fit.


## Unseemly Truth

Here's the truth: I am petty and trivial. I lack compassion. I'm a control freak who doesn't share well with others. I care more about a TV program than the feelings and interests of another person.

I am self-absorbed and envious. I'm a stealer of Sweet'N Low.

Years ago, my daughter, Laura, had commented that I don't curse, and I had to confess to her that I do curse inside my head. And once I threw a can of Pringles at her. Hard.

I have shoes in my closet that I've never worn (and I keep buying more); I rarely volunteer at church or anywhere else. When I'm not the center of attention, I get ticked. I secretly love hearing gossip.

One Christmas season I refused to put even a quarter in the Salvation Army kettle.

I could go on, but there isn't enough room to list all my sins and shortcomings.

❧

For years before she died, I had an ongoing, quite nasty debate with a woman who would take issue with me because I regularly confessed my sins and weaknesses in my weekly newspaper column.

She would call me "unseemly" and tell me that I was dishonoring the name of Christ. She would scold me and say I should write only about victory in Jesus and loving one another and keeping the commandments.

She thought that Christians should present a proper standard of living, that we shouldn't air our dirty laundry in public, because "what would people think?"

On the one hand I agree with my critic that there is victory in Jesus and that Christians should talk about the awesome deeds that God does in and through and for His people. But I also think that we need to tell the whole truth, the true truth, to each other and to those outside the faith who may be looking in, and that includes the not-so-victorious aspects of our lives as well.

## The Big Lie and the Big Truth

A friend of mine was recently on the receiving end of what she called "typical church people nastiness." She said, "I can see why the Romans used to throw Christians to the lions."

This friend works in a restaurant, and she often tells me that her least favorite customers are the Sunday after-church crowd.

I hate to admit it, but we Christians, especially when we're hungry, tend to get demanding and impatient.

My friend said that it infuriates her when she's busy and church people are being rude—and then in the middle of their rudeness they go into "witnessing mode," as she calls it, and will ask her, "Why aren't you in church, young lady?" or even, "If you died tonight, do you know for certain where you would spend eternity?"

Then they go back to being curt and rude, leave a meager tip and a gospel tract, and think they've shown Christ to some poor lost soul.

> *I hate to admit it, but we Christians, especially when we're hungry, tend to get demanding and impatient.*

My friend has told me, "If that's what Jesus does to a person, then I don't want anything to do with Christianity."

She has also said that she doesn't think she can be good enough to go to church.

That's the big lie—that only good people go to church.

But here's the big truth—only sinners are allowed in.

I may be wrong—but I don't think I am—I think that we Christians forget that there are only two kinds of people in the world: sinners who have run to Jesus to have their sin covered and sinners who haven't.

Those of us who have tend to forget that we're still sinners. We know that it's by grace and grace alone that we're made right with God to begin with, but we forget that it's also by grace alone that we live day by day.

So we try to do the Christian life by our own best efforts,

but we can't. However, because we think that everyone else can and does, we try to pretend that we can and do, too. We pretend that we're okay and that we "have the joy, joy, joy, joy down in our hearts" and talk about having the victory in Jesus, all the while secretly thinking that we've somehow missed something, that because there's sin in our hearts and un-victory in our lives, something's wrong and we'll never please God.

That kind of thinking makes us insecure.

> *That's the big lie—that only good people go to church. But here's the big truth—only sinners are allowed in.*

Sometimes, too, when we're busy forgetting that we live by grace and grace alone, we start thinking that our place in God's family somehow makes us better than those outside the family, as if we're there because of something good in us.

That kind of thinking makes us rude to waitresses and nasty to store clerks.

We're even nasty to each other. Someone once said of Christians that we're the only ones who shoot our wounded. Is it any wonder that those who watch us don't want anything to do with our message?

As a Christian, my challenge—my whole reason for being—is to present the gospel authentically, to be a walking illustration of the grace of God. But I can't do that by pretending that I'm good when I'm not. People see right through that, and that's how we Christians get labeled as hypocrites.

But if I'm real, if I live honestly, those watching will take notice, and right in the middle of my sin and struggle, they will see Jesus.

## Blessed Are the Messy, for They
## Shall Be Loved by God

The late Michael Yaconelli was a minister in California at a church "for people who don't like to go to church." He called himself a klutz in the kingdom of God and a spiritual nincompoop.

He had said that his church was filled with people who didn't have it all together. Some had been made to feel guilty by former churches because their faith couldn't heal their troubled marriages or cure their cancer. His congregation was filled with people who loved Jesus but couldn't seem to conquer their addictions or who had been told that "real" Christians don't get angry or depressed, don't doubt, don't resent their families, and don't have children who go astray.

He wrote *Messy Spirituality: God's Annoying Love for Imperfect People* for messy people, he said, to let them know that Jesus spent most of His time on earth with messy people and that they were some of His favorite folks—and that they still are.

I've been in a few churches, and they've all been filled with messy people, although not all will admit it. Most don't.

In most churches, messy people pretend they're all neatly fixed. They get dressed up on Sunday mornings, and even though they might snipe at each other in the car on the way to church and say hurtful things and think even more hurtful thoughts, by the time they reach the parking lot they're smiling.

Everything's fine.

Not because they've confessed their nastiness to one another, but because they think they're the only ones who aren't neatly fixed and they don't want anyone else to know they're really a mess.

*Jesus spent most of His time on earth with messy people, and they were some of His favorite folks.*

So, they meet and greet each other and ask, "How are you?" and they answer, "Fine, and you?"

But they're not fine. I'm not fine. None of us are fine, unless by fine you mean Fouled-up, Insecure, Neurotic, and Exhausted.

We're F.I.N.E. I'm F.I.N.E., you're F.I.N.E., your pastor's F.I.N.E., my pastor's F.I.N.E., even Billy Graham's F.I.N.E.

Still, we keep pretending that we're not F.I.N.E., that our lives are not broken.

Yaconelli wrote:

There is no room for pretending in the spiritual life. Unfortunately, in many religious circles, there exists an unwritten rule. Pretend. Act like God is in control when you don't believe He is. Give the impression everything is okay in your life when it's not. Pretend you believe when you doubt; hide your imperfections; maintain the image of a perfect marriage with healthy and well-adjusted children when your family is like any other normal dysfunctional family. And whatever you do, don't admit that you sin.

But we do sin, often and regularly. We are a mess, even those of us who belong to Jesus. We all have secrets and private struggles. Yaconelli said that the essence of messy spirituality is refusing to pretend, lie, or allow others to believe that we are something we are not.

*But they're not fine. I'm not fine. None of us are fine, unless by fine you mean Fouled-up, Insecure, Neurotic, and Exhausted.*

However, he said, those who stop pretending and start being real expose the pretending of everyone else, bursting the bubble of the "perfect Christian life."

Pretenders don't like being exposed.

But pretending is hard work. There are too many rules to follow. You're always looking over your shoulder to see who's watching, smiling when you don't feel like it, and saying, "Praise the Lord!" when you really want to swear like a drunken sailor.

Admitting that you're a mess is difficult if you've never done it before, but once you do and you experience the freedom it brings, I promise you'll never want to go back to pretending.

I'm fortunate or blessed or whatever you want to call it to belong to a church where the members feel the freedom to share their messes with one another. ("Oh, your kid's in jail? So's mine—let's pray.")

"Your messes are God's opportunities," Yaconelli wrote. "They're not what He shuns; they're where He meets you, opens your eyes to the fullness of His love and transforms you with His grace."

The good news of the gospel is that Jesus came to seek and to save imperfect, messy people and to turn their "messes into masterpieces."

It begins with confession.


## Welcome to the Confession Booth—Let the Healing Begin

When I was a child, the church I went to was dark and spooky, with lots of statues and stained glass and candles. Along the walls were what I thought were closets. Actually, they were confessionals, although I also thought that was where they kept the devil.

To me, confession was a scary thing, and not pleasant. First of all, I had a hard time thinking of sins to confess other than "I hit my little brother" or "I harbored bad thoughts."

Secondly, when I reached an age when I really understood sin, I wasn't about to blab it to some man behind a screen in the closet next to the one where I knelt and have him think I was a *sinner*. But I got used to it and just sort of bit the bullet and delivered my list of sins as fast as I could, grabbed my penance, and left.

I've since come to see confession not as a necessary chore because that's what Christians are supposed to do, but the gateway to a genuine sense of freedom.

People think confession is a bad thing. It's a hard thing, but it's not a bad thing. In the New Testament, James says to "Make this your common practice: Confess your sins to each other and pray for each other" (5:16, *The Message*).

That's difficult to do because pride and arrogance and self-protection get in the way. But James goes on to say, "Confess…so that you can live together whole and healed" (v. 16, *The Message*).

I love that, don't you? We confess so we can be made whole and healed, not humiliated. It makes confession a delight.

*People think confession is a bad thing.
It's a hard thing, but it's not a bad thing.*

In *Blue Like Jazz*, author Donald Miller writes about the time he attended Reed College in Portland, Oregon, a school that had once been selected by the *Princeton Review* as the college "where students are most likely to ignore God."

He writes about Ren Fayre, a yearly three-day festival where everybody gets drunk, high, and naked. Because Reed wasn't a hospitable place for Christianity, Miller and several Christian friends sometimes stayed in the closet about their faith.

But one year they decided it was time to make a statement

and that the perfect time to do it would be during Ren Fayre.

In the middle of all the sin and debauchery, these Christians decided that they would build a confession booth on campus and put up a sign: CONFESS YOUR SINS. The original plan was for festivalgoers to confess their sins to them, but then "Tony the Beat Poet" announced that instead they, the Christians, would confess to them, the non-Christians.

"We are going to confess that, as followers of Jesus, we have not been very loving," Tony told the group. "We have been bitter, and for that, we are sorry."

They agreed to apologize for the Crusades, for televangelists, for neglecting the poor and the lonely.

If I had been there, I would have added that I wanted to confess to stubbornly avoiding the Salvation Army kettle at Christmas and making a big, stinking deal about not being able to tape *Gilmore Girls*. It's not just the big, flashy sins that we are guilty of, but the petty, everyday sins. I might not ever drive a spear through a heathen who refuses to convert, but I will yell at my kids and make snarky comments to my friends about what people in the mall are wearing.

"We will ask them to forgive us," Tony said, "and we will tell them that in our selfishness, we have misrepresented Jesus on this campus. We will tell people who come into the booth that Jesus loves them."

Miller says that for much of his life he had defended Christianity because he thought that to admit that Christians had done wrong was to discredit Christ. But he discovered, just as I, too, have discovered, that the opposite is true, that when we Christians confess our sins and are real and honest about our struggles, we show how much we need Jesus. The right thing to do, Miller says, is to apologize for getting in the way of Jesus.

So this small band of believers erected a confession booth and put on monks' robes and invited people to come in to hear their confessions. As they confessed, the unbelievers started to listen. Some offered forgiveness; all were kind, Miller says.

Hours went by, and Miller was changed by the process. He had begun with doubts but came out believing so strongly in Jesus that he was ready to go out and die for his faith. It felt good to have gotten so much off his chest, and even more so, he felt at peace with God.

## The Rest of the Story

The true truth is that I am a mess. I am fouled-up, insecure, neurotic, and exhausted. I am first and foremost a sinner, but that's only half of the gospel message. The other half is this: Although we, the rescued, redeemed, and ransomed, will sometimes disappoint, sometimes offend, sometimes be rude to waitresses and snappy to store clerks, although we will rarely be what others think we should be and may never be what we want to be—pay attention now—if we are in Christ, God has changed us and will continue to change us.

Here's a promise you can take to the bank: If God starts a good work in you, He will finish it, and it will be perfect by the time He's done (Philippians 1:6, my paraphrase.).

> *I am first and foremost a sinner, but that's only half of the gospel message.*

Even though I'm not there yet, by God's grace, and grace alone, I am getting better. He has begun to make me patient, and often I am. He has begun to make me kind. I am less envious than I was, less boastful, less rude and self-seeking.

Things that used to annoy me don't. I am quick to forgive

because I've been forgiven, more lavish with my love because I've been loved, more generous with my money and my stuff because God has been generous and gracious to me.

It's true that I have far to go, but God has begun a good work in me, and He won't abandon what He's started. And because I am accepted by God solely based on my faith in Christ, no matter how far I fall, no matter how great my sin, no matter how far from perfect I am, I am forgiven, and He is and will continue to be well-pleased.

That, my friend, is the gospel that brings security and the freedom to tell the truth about who I really am: a sinner first and foremost, but one who is dearly loved.

And where does obeying the law of God fit into all this grace stuff, you ask? I'm glad you asked!

One of the biggest criticisms of those who teach and preach and write about grace is that we nullify and/or vilify God's law. Toss it aside. *That's so yesterday.*

Let me assure you, that is not what I think or feel or believe. The law is my delight, as King David said throughout the psalms. Whenever I read the shalts and shalt nots—the call to rid myself of anger, rage, malice, and slander; the command not to lie; and the charge to "clothe [myself] with compassion, kindness, humility, gentleness and patience" (Colossians 3:12)—my spirit and my soul, my mind and my heart cry out, "Yes! I want to do and be all that!"

> *It's true that I have far to go, but God has begun a good work in me, and He won't abandon what He's started.*

The freedom of grace is the freedom to try and do it, secure in knowing that even if I don't and can't do all that the law commands (which I can't humanly do even on my best day), I am still and always accepted by the Father—and forgiven even before I confess.

So, here's my invitation, which is really God's invitation: Let's make this our common practice, to confess our sins to each other and pray for each other so that we can live together whole and healed.

# Think on These Things

*Think:* What are some common criticisms that non-Christians have about Christians? In what ways are they true?

*Study:* Letting others know our true selves is scary—so why should we? (See 2 Corinthians 3:13–4:7; 5:18–20; 12:9–10.) Why can we tell the truth? (See Romans 8:1, 31–34.)

*Apply:* James 5:16 says, "Confess your sins to each other and pray for each other so that you may be healed." The Amplified Bible expands that to say: confess "your slips,  your false steps, your offenses, your sins" that you may be healed "and restored [to a spiritual tone of mind and heart]." Think of the ways you have pretended to be better than you are. If you have a friend whom you trust, begin telling the truth "that you may be healed."

*Consider:* On his radio broadcast, *Key Life*, Steve Brown said, "Church isn't for good people who are getting better. It's for bad people who know they can't get any better by trying. Sometimes they do get better, but that's not the point of going to church. Getting loved by God is the point…and obedience will follow. But getting loved by God is first."

What would church be like if its members stopped pretending to be good and came together just to be loved by God first? How attractive would that be to outsiders? How can you begin to make that happen?

*Meditate:* "Every morning I vow to love thee more fervently, to serve thee more sincerely, to be more devoted in my life, to be wholly thine; yet I soon stumble, backslide, and have to confess my weakness, misery, and sin. But I bless thee that the finished work of Jesus needs no addition from my doings, that his oblation is sufficient satisfaction for my sin." —taken from a Puritan prayer from *The Valley of Vision*

# Chapter Eleven

# When Pigs Fly

## When you've glimpsed hope

*Hope to the last…. Always hope….*
*Don't leave off hoping, or it's no use doing anything.*
*Hope, hope, to the last!*
Charles Dickens, *Nicholas Nickleby*

O n Christmas Eve 2004 I saw a pig fly. At first I wasn't sure, because it wasn't in full flight. It was more like this pig that I had been wanting to see fly had sprouted wings and was taxiing down the runway, readying for takeoff.

Now that I've said that, I haven't decided yet if I'm going to tell you what my "pig" is. It's deeply personal and involves another person, so let's just say that it's something I'd wanted to see God do for a very long time. It had been so long that I had begun to think it would happen only "when pigs fly."

In other words, never.

I still might tell you, but for now I'm choosing to be vague so you can take the thing that you want God to do and insert it into my story, thus making it your story. That way, maybe you will be encouraged to believe that God truly can do what you think is impossible.

But before I go any further, I have a confession to make. When it comes to faith and hope and believing, I am not the person you want to listen to. That would be Charlie Wade.

Charlie owns the bike shop about a half mile from my house. He calls himself a closet Pentecostal and loves to read books by Brennan Manning and Thomas Merton, and he loves to pray.

I call Charlie a "raving optimist," which is a nice way of calling him a lunatic. He believes that the impossible can and does happen, and even though I've written two books about prayer, Charlie actually prays and believes that God can and will answer his prayers. If he prays for rain, he brings an umbrella.

Although I believe God can and does answer prayer, if I pray for rain, I tend to leave my umbrella at home, if you know what I mean.

A few years ago, Charlie's grandson developed a rare condition that caused his head to jerk involuntarily. It baffled the doctors and saddened his family—there's no known cure for this condition.

So, being the optimist that he is, Charlie made a list of all the places in the Bible where Jesus had healed a child. Next, Charlie set out to use those Scriptures in his daily prayers, believing without a tinge of doubt that God would heal his grandson.

That drove me, the raving skeptic, crazy.

*Although I believe God can and does answer prayer,*
*if I pray for rain, I tend to leave my*
*umbrella at home, if you know what I mean.*

"What if God doesn't heal your grandson?" I asked Charlie. Not that I think God can't or won't answer prayer, just that sometimes He doesn't heal when we ask, no matter how strong our faith.

Charlie says this is where he and I are diametrical opposites.

Wouldn't you know it, after a few months of praying, Charlie's grandson's head jerking stopped. Charlie said that God had healed the boy—as a direct answer to his prayers. "I believe it with all my heart," he said.

I believe that God healed the little boy, too. "But would it have happened if you hadn't prayed?" I asked Charlie after he told me about it.

He says I drive him crazy.

But being a raving skeptic has its advantages, such as being placed on a raving optimist's daily prayer list. Charlie prays for me every morning, which is a good thing, because Lord knows I need all the prayer I can get. And because I'm on his prayer list, I tell him about this thing that I want God to do. Sometimes when we talk about it, he'll laugh and tell me how he can see it happening "without a doubt, no ifs, ands, or buts."

When he's done prattling on about faith and hope and all that, I'll just say, "Yeah, yeah. When pigs fly."

## Deep-Fat, Turkey-Fried Hope

Still, there's something about hope that even the most raving skeptic can't deny, as if God Himself plants it deep inside His people. Like a compass that points North, hope within points us heavenward, whether we know it or not. That's what I think, anyway.

For example, take the time a few years ago that I ate dinner with the group of people I call my life group, a bunch of friends from my church who all live in the same town as I do. We're like a minichurch within the bigger church. We get together twice a month for dinner; this time it was for a pre-Christmas party.

Harriet, as always, brought a pot of green beans with bacon. Somebody brought a purple dessert, and someone else brought a brown one. One of the Karens—we have several—disguised mashed yellow squash with sour cream and some other stuff that made me forget I was eating squash, it was that good.

> *There's something about hope that even the most raving skeptic can't deny, as if God Himself plants it deep inside His people.*

I didn't really want to go to this dinner that night. My husband was away and I was lonely and felt like feeling sorry for myself (sniff, sniff). However, I was also hungry and didn't feel like cooking.

So I went for the food, but I left with hope.

Whenever our life group gets together, there are always too many people for us all to sit at one table, or even in the same room, so I never know who I'll be eating with or what the topic of conversation will be. Sometimes we talk about the finer points of theology, but mostly we talk about regular stuff.

That night we talked about deep-frying turkeys.

The guys at the table got all googly-eyed talking about all the turkey-frying gadgets and gizmos at the Home Depot, and then someone wondered about the legality of deep-frying the pesky sandhill cranes that wander our neighborhoods. Then we talked about which dessert we liked better—the purple or the brown. (It was a tie.)

I kept thinking that Jesus would've had a good time at our table that night, and I thought that He probably would've been a deep-fat turkey fryer Himself. We know He roasted fish.

After dinner we had a gift exchange. There were some boxes of candy, an apron, a Santa hat that had "I believe in Jesus" written on it. The wisest man in our group ironically got a book about wisdom.

I got a book about hope.

I've said it before, I think God must have a great time being God, and He probably gets a huge kick out of knocking the skepticism out of His doubting children. Just about the time you think hope is gone, or at least out of your reach, and you're about to give up and give in and buy a bunch of cats and never come out of your house because *why bother?*—*besides*, you think, *why would God care about the stuff that keeps me awake at night?*—just when you start to think that hope is for chumps, that's when God goes and plops hope in your lap and proves you wrong about it and about Him.

The rule at the gift exchange was that when it came your turn to unwrap a gift, you could forcibly trade with someone whose gift you wanted. I hid mine behind my back. I hadn't realized how badly I needed it and didn't want anyone taking my hope away from me. Someone came close, but I threatened to deep-fat fry her like a turkey.

You do that when someone tries to rob you of your hope.

Sometimes people get themselves into situations or life just happens to them, and it looks like hope got stuffed in a sock drawer somewhere or tossed out with the trash—or stolen out from under them. When you think hope is gone, you think you can't go on. That's why I clung to mine.

There's a proverb that says, "Hope deferred makes the heart sick" (Proverbs 13:12). I wasn't anywhere near the heartsick point that night, but I have been. At one point during my husband's depression my heart was sick and I knew it—and that's when God came to me in a whisper, supernaturally, healingly, hope-fully, letting me know that He was and is and that I could trust Him.

After we finished exchanging gifts we talked about the year gone by. Bob, whose home we invade for these dinners, talked about it being a roller-coaster year. He said some of us who were way, way down the previous year were way, way up that year. I think I was somewhere in the middle, but on the downish side.

Some of us got teary thinking about the down times and then teary again because not one of us had had our hope stolen away. God had been good through even the worst of the bad.

It's during the worst of the bad that you need hope most.

Working for a newspaper, I hear of a lot of "worst of the bad," and sometimes it's enough to make you go crazy, unless or until God reminds you that He is the God of hope.

The apostle Paul prayed for the people in the church in Rome that the God of hope would fill them with "all joy and peace" as they trusted in Him so that they might "overflow with hope by the power of the Holy Spirit" (Romans 15:13).

God's people, me included, would do well to memorize that and hold on to it. There is a lot of worst of the bad out there. I hope it doesn't happen, but if it does, I'm going to need hope.

*It's during the worst of the bad that you need hope most.*

## The Face of Hope

If hope has a face, it would be that of Alissa Kussman. Every time the doctors have told her parents, "There's no hope," she has proved them wrong.

The youngest of six children, she was Jenny and Peter Kussmans' "surprise" baby. Before then the family was living well and wanted for nothing. When Alissa was at twenty-four weeks gestation, the doctors discovered that the baby's lungs were under-developed and advised an abortion, which the Kussmans refused.

Then Peter lost his job, including health insurance. As medical bills mounted, they mortgaged their house. They had one vehicle repossessed, and the other one broke down and they couldn't afford to get it fixed. On top of that, Jenny developed gestational diabetes.

At thirty-six weeks gestation, an amniocentesis caused Jenny to go into labor. Next, an epidural caused her heart and lungs to weaken, which stopped the baby's heartbeat altogether. The doctors told the Kussmans to prepare for a stillborn baby, so they did.

As everyone in the delivery room held their breath in sorrow mixed with a distant hope, the little girl cried.

The Kussmans considered it a miracle and brought their tiny, five-pound baby home. All was well for six weeks, and then Alissa stopped breathing. Over the next year that became a common occurrence, resulting in the baby spending more time in the hospital than at home.

Meanwhile, the doctors discovered that she had no thymus gland; she had acid reflux disease, which required surgery to tie off her stomach; she needed a heart and lung transplant; and she had a rare bone syndrome causing malformed kneecaps, and she is without wrists.

"The doctors said she wouldn't crawl, but she did," Jenny said just before Alissa's first birthday. "They said she wouldn't walk, but she's trying it on her own. She had pneumonia; she had surgery on her throat to help her breathe. They said there was an 80 percent chance that she wouldn't talk because of damage to her vocal chords, but after four weeks she was yelling."

Alissa Kussman will most likely always have medical problems, and the Kussmans admitted that they still have times when they feel hopeless. However, they also said that all they have to do is look at Alissa's bright eyes and hear her laugh to know that God is who He says He is, a God of hope.

## When Hope Dies

As seemingly hopeless as the Kussmans' situation may have been, it wasn't anything compared to the hopelessness felt by Martha of Bethany, one of the women who followed Jesus.

Jesus loved Martha as well as her sister, Mary, and brother, Lazarus. I mentioned him earlier.

Anyway, Jesus hung out with them, ate with them, taught His disciples in Martha's living room.

I imagine Martha listening to Jesus, noticing how His words brought life to the Scriptures, how He brought life to everyone who listened to Him and believed, how He brought life to her. He wasn't like the other teachers who quoted this rabbi or that rabbi. Jesus spoke truth as if He was truth itself.

As if He was hope itself—the hope of Israel, the One the Scriptures promised would come and redeem them, the One they had hoped for and longed for and been waiting for. Nothing could go wrong as long as Jesus was around, Martha probably thought. Or if it did, He would fix it.

How could He not?

Then Lazarus got sick. Martha and Mary cared for him, prayed and hoped that he would get well. But as hard as they prayed, Lazarus didn't get any better, so Martha did the only thing that she knew would get the job done—she sent for Jesus, who was out of town. She knew He would drop everything and rush right over and Lazarus would immediately get well. Jesus did stuff like that all the time, so why wouldn't He do it for her?

But when Jesus heard about Lazarus, He did nothing. He told

His disciples, "This sickness will not end in death. No, it is for God's glory so that God's Son may be glorified through it" (John 11:4). Then He stayed where He was for two more days.

What would you think if you were Martha? I would vacillate between being frantic with worry that Jesus wouldn't get there in time and confident beyond confidence that my dear friend, the promised Messiah, the One I had fed and entertained and believed in, would surely come through.

But He didn't.

She had waited and hoped, and as Lazarus breathed his last, as she and Mary wrapped their dear brother in grave clothes, placed him in a tomb, and sealed it, as they grieved the one they loved, Martha had to face the truth: Jesus had failed her. The One she had put her hope in had let her down.

Can you imagine her pain? Not just in losing her brother, but in losing her hope. Her grief was not just because of Lazarus, but also because Jesus didn't come to her aid when she had hoped that He would.

The other day, a friend asked if I had ever been angry at God—not just miffed, but so furiously angry that I could spit tacks. So angry that if I met God in an alley, I just might try to beat Him to a bloody pulp.

"Yeah," I said. "I've been that angry."

Sometimes, in the seemingly hopeless situations when life stinks so badly that it makes you nearly insane, you forget that God is good and all-mighty, that He's Almighty, and that He's just. You forget that His ways are so much higher than ours and that He knows exactly what He's about and that He will never leave His own helpless and hopeless and peaceless.

*You forget that His ways are so much higher than ours.*

But sometimes, like when you've just buried your brother, you forget and you think, *God, if this is how You treat Your friends, then I'm certainly glad I'm not an enemy.* That's when you need hope to remind you that God still is and that even if you want to punch Him in the nose, He won't ever leave you or forsake you, even if it feels like it sometimes.

I bet that's how Martha felt when she saw Jesus walking up the road, four days after Lazarus had died. I bet she wanted to throw shoes at Jesus for disappointing her, but at the same time, I bet the hope compass within her kept her from it. Maybe she resigned herself to thinking, *There's always eternity. I'll wait until I see my brother then.*

Although Martha didn't know this at the time, Jesus already knew that Lazarus had died, and He had even told His disciples.

When she ran to meet Him, she cried, "Lord, if you had been here, my brother would not have died." If I were her, I might have added, "Where were You? You were my only hope, and now it's too late!"

## Hope Makes Pigs Fly

As Jesus and Martha talked on the road about the death of Lazarus, they talked about the hope of the final resurrection, when all the dead are raised to life at the end of the world.

"Your brother will be raised up," Jesus said.

"I know that he will be raised up in the resurrection at the end of time," she replied.

"You don't have to wait for the End," Jesus said. "I am, right now, Resurrection and Life. The one who believes in me, even though he or she dies, will live. And everyone who lives believing in me does not ultimately die at all. Do you believe this?"

"Yes, Master," Martha said. "All along I have believed that you are the Messiah, the Son of God who comes into the world" (John 11:23–27, *The Message*).

Another Bible translation records Martha saying, "Yes, Lord! I believe that you are Christ, the Son of God. You are the one we hoped would come into the world" (CEV).

Martha didn't say anything about her disappointment. Instead, she followed Jesus to her brother's grave and watched as He wept—and then as He ordered the stone seal to be removed from the tomb.

"Didn't I tell you that if you believed, you would see the glory of God?" Jesus told Martha. Next, He called Lazarus's name and told him to come out—and the dead man did. When Jesus calls your name, you respond, even if you're dead.

I would like to have been Martha at that moment. I would like to have been Jesus. When I get to heaven, if I remember, I'll have to ask them what was going on in their minds just then. It must have been one roller-coaster ride that day.

As I see it, hope has a bite to it. It's like this bottle of salad dressing called Oriental Sweet Heat that I found at the market recently. I had wanted to make a shredded carrot and dried cranberry salad, but with a kick to it, so, I used this dressing that's both sweet and spicy-hot.

It reminded me of my husband's depression, which was "hot." It was painful, and I burned inside with grief and helplessness as I would sit out on the dock by our house and cry. I felt helpless because my husband felt hopeless.

Then as a breeze would blow across my face, as if God Himself was there—and He was—it was sweet, although I kept crying.

*Hope isn't hope until it's all you've got left.*

I've heard it said that real hope isn't hope until everything around you is hopeless. Hope isn't hope until it's all you've got left. You've got to have the bite in order to appreciate the sweetness.

Sometimes, but not too often, God raises a brother back to life, or He heals a baby that the doctors say can't be healed. Mostly, He sends books and breezes and Scripture promises and songs. Mostly, He makes pigs fly.

## Rustling of Pigs' Wings

At the beginning of 2004 I had asked God if I could see a pig fly. I didn't think He would show me one, but at the end of the year, on Christmas Eve, He did.

It wasn't as dramatic as a dead man coming back to life, or even a baby proving the doctors wrong. Not all situations that you need hope for are that dire and desperate. But hope is still hope, and people still need it—and God still gives it.

A longtime friend I had been praying for, who hadn't been to church for years and years and who I doubted ever would, showed up on Christmas Eve to surprise me. Just like that, out of the blue, no phone call to warn me, no advance notice.

At first I laughed when I saw my friend because I was so shocked, but not really. All throughout the year God had been sending me pig sightings—I'd see an ad in the paper with a picture of a flying pig; one day I went to a woman's house, and I saw a ceramic pig with wings high up on a bookshelf. Even in an episode of *Law & Order*, one of the detectives mumbled, "What do you know—pigs do fly."

With each "sighting" I would think of my longtime friend, and then I would imagine Charlie at the bike shop saying, "God's going to make that pig of yours fly, without a doubt, no ifs, ands, or buts," and I would just shake my raving skeptical head.

So I laughed when I saw my friend walk into church, but then I stopped short and stood amazed.

Then I worshiped.

That's what you do when you see a pig fly. After you stare at it in a combination of belief-disbelief, once you rub your eyes and pinch yourself to see if you're awake or asleep and dreaming, after you laugh because this is what you had hoped for and you can't believe it's happening right in front of you—you worship.

You worship the God who is faithful and creative and who delights in doing the impossible when you least expect it. You worship because the God of hope has filled you with all joy and peace as you trust in Him so that you may overflow with hope by the power of the Holy Spirit.

When you see a pig fly, you worship because God has humbled Himself and answered your prayers, reminding you that you are His and that even if you disbelieve His willingness, even if you get angry and want to punch Him in the nose, you will always be His child and He will never leave you nor forsake you.

I had known that God can do anything, but when it came to believing that He actually would do something I deeply wanted, I had said, "When pigs fly," and one did. Like I said, it wasn't in full flight, but I heard and I felt and I saw the rustling of wings. Full-flighted hope was still distant, but God had given me enough to keep trusting, keep believing, keep hoping.

And so, although it may often be reluctantly, I will.

*You worship the God who is faithful and creative and who delights in doing the impossible when you least expect it.*

# *Think on These Things*

*Think:* What does it mean to have hope? Is there any situation for which you lack hope? In what areas of your life are you most hopeful? What is your hope based on?

*Study:* Read Romans 8, and note every verse or thought that inspires hope or encouragement in you. Read also: Lamentations 3:18–26; Romans 4:18–21; 5:1–5; Ephesians 1:18–19; 1 Peter 1:21.

*Apply:* What keeps you awake at night? Take one or more of the verses about hope that you just read, and ask God how His words about hope can apply to your situation—in other words, how can they be your hope?

*Consider:* Lamentations 3:22–23 says, "Because of the LORD's great love we are not consumed, for his compassions never fail. They are new every morning; great is [his] faithfulness." How can believing this help you to sleep at night?

*Meditate:* "Praise be to the God and Father of our Lord Jesus Christ! In his great mercy he has given us new birth into a living hope through the resurrection of Jesus Christ from the dead, and into an inheritance that can never perish, spoil or fade—kept in heaven for you." —1 Peter 1:3–4

# Chapter Twelve

# Song of the God-Struck

When you've grasped grace

*Without worship you shrink; it's as brutal as that.*
PETER SHAFFER, *EQUUS*

As I write this, I'm sitting in the darkened sanctuary of my church, pen in hand, a yellow legal pad on my lap. It's a Friday morning, and it's quiet. I'm here to meet with God. To write, to pray, to think, to worship.

I love my church. On the outside it's stately, massive, and majestic. Modern French Gothic, I think it's called. You walk in through huge glass doors, and the first thing you do is look up at the cathedral ceilings and the glass and the plain cement walls. It's mouth-dropping simple and nothing short of amazing.

The inside, before you get to the sanctuary, looks like a hotel lobby, with overstuffed leather sofas and chair groupings. It looks like a place where you would want to hang out. That's the way we as a congregation designed it. That's the way we thought our Father would like it—a place where His kids could come and hang out, maybe play checkers at the bistro tables, laugh or cry together on the sofas.

Sometimes some of us get together—there are about fourteen hundred of us in all—and we sprawl out on the floor or wherever we can find a spot and eat pizza or cookies. When that happens, it's quite noisy and messy and chaotic. It's quite familyish—and quite holy.

Just like it's holy here in the sanctuary this quiet Friday morning with the sun in the eastern sky shining through the overhead arched window as my only light while I sit in wonder and awe.

How did I get here? Who is God that He should choose and call me, change me, turn my life upside down and inside out, that He should bless me beyond my highest, deepest, widest dreams? Who is He that I would rise early just to come and sit in His quiet and dare believe that He will meet me here—me, the one who loves Him so meagerly?

A cloud passes across the sun, hiding its light from me. Sometimes I think that's true of God as well, that He hides Himself. Maybe He does, but maybe it's more like the clouds that block the warmth and the light, the radiance and the beauty and the glory. After all, the sun doesn't move; it stays right there, outside the window, reaching down to where I sit.

Through the prophet Isaiah, God said, "In repentance and rest is your salvation, in quietness and trust is your strength" (Isaiah 30:15). There's no TV here to distract me; I've even turned off my phone. The world can wait while I am here in my Father's house, still and at rest.

King David said, "I was glad when they said to me, 'Let us go to the house of the LORD'" (Psalm 122:1, NASB). It's good when God's house is filled with His people, and it's good—it is very good—when God's house is filled only with Himself.

And me.

As I sit here, my emotions flit: from captivated awe to head-scratching wonder and then to a deep sadness because of the many who don't think of God's house as a good place to be. I used to think that, but now I don't. Now I can't think of any place on earth I'd rather be.

*If you don't love coming to His house,
then you haven't met the living God.*

My pastor says that when you meet the living God, you find healing in the deepest parts of you. So I guess if you simply go to church on Sunday mornings and you don't walk away healed at your core, and if you don't love coming to His house, then you haven't met the living God.

## Body and Blood in Aluminum Cups—and Methodist Sheep

As part of my job at the newspaper covering religion in my community, I get to attend all kinds of religious services. Some are dry as toast and some are quite lively and some are so devoid of the living God that I wonder why the people even bother to meet. But all make me think, and God has a way of going with me and revealing something of Himself to me.

When Pope John Paul II died and it seemed like everyone wanted to be Catholic, if only for a week, I thought I would revisit my own Catholic roots and went to a weekday Mass. I arrived late, but got caught up quickly enough as the priest held up the large round Eucharist host for all to see.

"The body of Christ," he told us.

When I was little, I used to take slices of soft, gooey Wonder Bread and smash them, then bite the edges until it made circles and pretend they were Communion hosts. The body of Christ in a polka-dotted plastic bread bag.

Next the priest held up the cup of wine.

When I was little, I used Kool-Aid to play Communion. The blood of Christ in shiny aluminum cups.

Then the priest sang, "Let us proclaim the mystery of our faith: Christ has died. Christ is risen. Christ will come again."

*Has died. Is risen. Will come again*, I thought. How awesome is that?

Some churches have Communion every week, but mine doesn't. Consequently, when we do, it takes on weight, at least in my mind. My pastor always asks us to come to Communion soberly. We are there to remember the Lord's sacrificial death.

At one point during Communion at my church, the sanctuary gets quiet, as quiet as it is right now. The pastor instructs us to examine ourselves, to think about our sin and our need, but not to drum up worthiness. Instead, we're to experience grace and then respond with gratitude and thanksgiving.

> *We're to experience grace and then respond with gratitude and thanksgiving.*

I always know that, but sometimes I forget. Sometimes I forget it so deeply that I've actually skipped church to avoid Communion.

I remember one Sunday morning. I had every intention of going to church, but about three miles from home, when I should have gone straight, I turned left instead.

I had been thinking about sheep. Earlier in the week I had visited with an Episcopal priest who collects stuffed toy sheep, including a group of them that he calls his "Methodist" sheep.

He said you could tell they're Methodist because they have smiles, and Methodists always smile.

So I turned left and headed for the Methodist church.

The Episcopal priest was right—the Methodists were smiling.

And then came Communion. That's when I heard the Shepherd of wandering sheep call my name, but not before I heard Him laugh. If you've never heard God laugh—Father, Son, and Holy Ghost busting a gut—then you haven't heard the music of heaven. I had gone to the Methodist church hoping to escape Communion at my church, only to run smack into Communion there. It was as if God was saying, "Gotcha!"

As I've said before, I think God has a good time being God.

Then came "examination" time, and I didn't like what I found, but then I remembered that the Shepherd had already taken care of it. "The good shepherd lays down his life for the sheep," Jesus had said to His disciples (John 10:11).

At that Methodist church, those taking Communion get out of their seats to go to the front. They take a pinch of bread from a broken loaf and dip it into the goblet of grape juice. The minister holding the bread said, "This is the body of Christ, broken for you."

At that moment, maybe unlike any other time before, I knew how true that was.

Then as I dipped my bread into the grape juice the minister said, "This is the blood of Christ, poured out for you."

Oh, how I knew that it was!

I can't say that I had a grand epiphany or revelation or broke down sobbing just then, but the living God had met me and healed something in the deepest part of me and I smiled—like a Methodist. The Shepherd had come looking for His wandering sheep. He knew that she was wandering from experiencing Communion with Him, so He brought Communion to her.

At my church we say that Communion is a sacrament, a means of grace. Grace meaning undeserved favor. Grace meaning that through Communion Christ gives us strength and draws us closer to Himself. Grace meaning that when a sheep goes wandering, the Shepherd goes to get it. Not to condemn or punish, but to rescue and to love.

That's what I'm thinking about on this Friday morning, here in the darkened sanctuary of my church.

## Walking to Heaven Together

Although it's quiet right now, you should've been here a few weeks ago on a Wednesday night. A couple hundred of us, most wearing shorts and flip-flops, were hanging out in the lobby area, eating, of course.

Earlier, before most of the folks got there, some kid in a red T-shirt was running around—one of Blair and Sheri Commons' boys I think—and I was stretched out on one of the sofas listening to Angela Vick singing, "Who would've thought that a Lamb could rescue the souls of men."

I love that song and love the way Angela sings it. She could sing a grocery list and make it sound good.

Then Ray Cardinali peered over the back of the sofa and asked if I was comfortable.

"Yes, I am," I told him. "I am in my Father's house, in His front room. My shoes are off, and I am comfortable in His presence."

Ray laughed, the boy in the red T-shirt ran, Angela sang, and I thought, *Now this is church.*

Like I said, you should've been there; I think you would've liked it.

Later, Mike Bennett told me about his huge extended family and how great it is when everyone comes home. He said there are so many people in his family, with about a dozen birthdays in August alone, that they've decided not to buy each other birthday presents but have family barbecues instead.

I know he was talking about the Bennetts, but he was describing the church and how great it is when everyone comes to our Father's house.

My uncle-dad says that God saves people in bunches. My pastor says that we walk to heaven together. I'm glad, too. Life is too difficult to do it alone, and it's too sweet not to share it.

*Life is too difficult to do it alone, and it's too sweet not to share it.*

Last Sunday morning—I think I was sitting in this same exact place—I looked around the sanctuary before the service started and thought, *Who are all these people?* We, as a church, are a motley bunch, yet we are all so comfortable in this place.

The sanctuary roof leaks, so we've set out buckets to catch the drips, which I find oddly endearing. I find the people endearing as well: Charlotte and Harry, who sit behind me each week and get there at least a half hour early; Harriet Eich, who likes to wear hats and bright colors and isn't afraid to speak her mind.

There's Ryan, both arms covered in tattoos, who's an intern at a local homeless shelter; Charlie Wade, who sends me e-mails and books to read; Bill Ward is hard of hearing, so when you talk to him you have to yell. When Bill likes something the pastor says in his sermon, he holds his hand up at about shoulder height and nods his fist as if to say, "Right on, brother."

Sam Miller used to grow roses. He was a doctor around here a long time ago, and he and his wife, Garnet, founded our church. Garnet's in a nursing home now, and until he died earlier this year, Sam visited Garnet every day. I still love Sam, and I love my church.

Lots of people don't love church, don't even like it, and a lot of churches give them good reason not to. Author Philip Yancey grew up in a church that he didn't like, filled with unyielding rules and unspoken codes. I would bet his church wasn't a place where the people sat on the floor and ate pizza or stretched out on the sofas or played checkers at the bistro tables.

*Lots of people don't love church, don't even like it, and a lot of churches give them good reason not to.*

Yancey said that when he was old enough to do so, he walked away. Not so much away from Jesus as away from the church. Several years ago he wrote a book, *Church: Why Bother?* He wrote about how far many churches are from God's ideal. As he tried out metaphors for what a church should be, he thought of a neighborhood bar, a hangout "where everybody knows your name and they're always glad you came."

He said that the church should be a place for people "who know all about your lousy boss, your mother with heart trouble back in North Carolina, and the teenager who won't do what you tell him; a place where you can unwind, spill your life story, and get a sympathetic look, not a self-righteous leer."

Here in the quiet, as I think about my church, this group of mismatched-yet-handpicked oddballs and screwups, I think that God has an amazing sense of humor. I also think about George Lazo, who died about eight years ago. He played the trumpet and was an alcoholic most of his life and a Christian for only the last few years. At one time he hopped freight trains and lived in cardboard boxes.

I'm not sure how he died, cancer maybe, but I do remember how some of the members of my church decided that George would not die alone, and they took turns sitting with him around the clock until his final breath. The same thing when Harold Eich died. The same thing when any of us die. We are God's family; He placed us together to live with and love one another and to walk to heaven together.

That's my church. That's *the* church, God's church.

It's not a place of rigid rules and impossible edicts, at least it shouldn't be. Instead, it should be a place where doctors, door hangers, and struggling moms with squirmy toddlers, where sex addicts, retirees on social security, lonely widows, and Mary Kay salesladies can all come and just hang with each other and munch pizza on a breezy Wednesday night or worship together on a Sunday morning.

It should be a place where the gospel is preached and lived out through people whose lives have been made brand new, where sinners stand with sinners and seek forgiveness together.

It should be a place where it's okay to be who you are as you wait for God to complete His holy work that He started in you, a place where you can find people who will sit with you and hold your hand until you breathe your last breath.

St. Celsus once said, "These Christians love each other even before they are acquainted." I agree—sometimes when I think of these people whom I love even before I know them, sometimes, like right now as I write this, I love them and this place—leaky roof and all—so much that it hurts, but it's a good hurt.

## Here I Am to Worship

So here I am, with this good hurt, sitting in the quiet of my Father's house, feeling like I should remove my shoes, but not like that Wednesday night when I kicked them off to stretch out on the sofa.

This is different. I'm feeling a sense of anticipation. Of wonder and a bit of fear.

My thoughts drift to the words I once read that were written on the gymnasium wall of a Baptist church in Titusville, Florida. Taken from the *Westminster Catechism*, they said: "The chief end of man is to glorify God and enjoy Him forever."

I've been to some worship services where everyone looks like they suck lemons, as if they believe that the chief end of man is to look highbrow and fake-holy, as if worshiping the living God were something to be endured, not enjoyed.

But even those who have tasted what it means to enjoy God, sometimes, like when you've belonged to God for a while and your faith becomes stagnant and dry, worship isn't worship anymore—even if you continue going to church, even if when the music starts your arms automatically raise, even if you close your eyes, even if you sway as you sing.

Even if you appear to be worshiping, if your faith is stagnant, what might look like worship is more like an autopilot thing than anything else.

But if you're God's, even if you're far from where you ought to be, because you're His, He doesn't let you stay on autopilot forever. His Spirit within you continually stirs and prods you upward and forward, continually urging you, along with all of God's people, toward worship, the very thing for which we were created—it is our chief end.

And because God doesn't want us to miss out on the reason we are here and the enjoyment He wants to share with us, His Spirit stirs us to look up, look outward, to stand in awed amazement.

To worship.

We worship publicly, in community, as a church, walking to heaven together, and in rare, private moments, we worship alone, like I'm doing today.

As the sun shines on my face, I arise and stand in the beam of light beneath the window at the far end of the sanctuary, watching the flecks of—what is it? dust? holiness?—swirl about me. I have been a Christian for nearly thirty years, more than half of my life, but sometimes I think I haven't yet learned what it means to worship.

*sometimes I think I haven't yet learned what it means to worship.*

I look up at the big, arched window and study the red metal beams that form a cross. I can't take my eyes away from it. My shoes are off—I am standing on holy ground.

Author Max Lucado says worship happens when you become aware that "what you've been given is far greater than what you can give" and the awareness that "were it not for his touch, you'd still be hobbling and hurting, bitter and broken." He likens it to the "half-glazed expression on the parched face of a desert pilgrim as he discovers that the oasis is not a mirage."

I'm having such a moment as I blurt out into the quiet, "Why me, Lord? Why would You choose to rescue me?"

I am awestruck—I am God-struck as I call out, "Who *are* You?"

Then I answer my own question.

"You are the One my heart longs for, yet the One from whom I run. You are strange and other, terrifying and huge. You are holy, You are majestic, You are mighty, You are great.

"You tell the wind and the waves to be still, and they are. You created the mountains and the oceans and the galaxies—and You created me.

"Father, I'm not good, but I'm Yours. I don't understand it, but I'm glad. So utterly grateful and so very, very glad."

❧

As I stand in God's presence, I don't know if I should laugh or cry—so I do both. And then I sing:

> Let us love, and sing, and wonder,
> let us praise the Savior's name!
> He has hushed the law's loud thunder,
> He has quenched Mount Sinai's flame;
> He has washed us with his blood; he has washed us with
> his blood,
> He has washed us with his blood; he has brought us
> nigh to God.

I sing:

> Who would've thought that a Lamb could rescue the
> souls of men?

My pastor says that true worship is receiving the Father's love, as demonstrated by the death of His Son, and then responding to it.

"You don't worship to get His love," he says. "You can't conjure up His love. But if you've been rescued and redeemed and if you've experienced the Father's love, then you *will* worship."

So I do.

I think about the bread and the wine and the mystery of our faith: Christ has died. Christ is risen. Christ will come again—and I worship.

I think about the people who will come and fill up these pews on Sunday morning and about the light that shines through the window and the light that shines through our dark, dark world—and I worship.

As I do, as I stand in God's presence, in His house, in His holy sanctuary, I am more alive, more like myself, more like who I was created to be than I've ever been before.

And I feel God smile.

# Think on These Things

*Think:* Worship is ascribing worth and value to someone or something. To what or to whom do we as a society ascribe worth? What makes them "worthy"?

*Study:* What are the elements of biblical worship? Take the following Scriptures, and use them to answer the questions regarding biblical worship: who, how, why, where, and when?

First Chronicles 16:29; Psalm 29:2; 95; 96; Malachi 3:10; John 4:23; Acts 2:42–47.

*Apply:* Make a list of the attributes or qualities of God, and use it as a basis of your worship.

*Consider:* Worship is instinctive—everybody worships something (Romans 1:25). Think about what you ascribe great worth to. How worthy is the object of your highest affections?

*Meditate:* "Weak is the effort of my heart and cold my warmest thought; but when I see Thee as Thou art, I'll praise Thee as I ought." —John Newton, "How Sweet the Name of Jesus Sounds"